Contents

Introduction

■ ■ ■

Content Guidance

■ ■ ■

Questions & Answers

D1353045

Introduction

Aims of the unit

Unit 2 in the new CCEA® GCE specification is worth 25% of the total A-level and 50% of the AS.

Questions require you to provide responses that clearly answer the question. To gain top marks, you need to provide detailed evidence to support your arguments. This evidence will usually come in the form of examples. There needs to be a clear link between the evidence and the argument.

Historiography or contemporary interpretations may also be used, but these are not required in this unit. Top marks can be gained without them.

You will have 45 minutes to answer each question. Each question contains an 8-mark part (Part (i)) and a 22-mark part (Part (ii)). In total, the examination will last 1 hour and 30 minutes. In this time it will be impossible to cover every single relevant detail that will address the question. Top-level marks will be awarded to those responses which cover most of the key issues, with clear evidence given to support the points that are made.

'Russia, 1903–1941' is Option 5 of the Unit 2 paper. The examination will require you to answer two questions out of four. This does not mean, however, that candidates can rely on simply revising only two topics, as questions may not come up in a way that suits them. It is better for candidates to give themselves as wide a choice of questions as possible.

The examination paper

The examination paper contains a variety of topics. Questions may cover more than one topic. Part (i), for example, might be on Bolshevik culture, while Part (ii) might be on the Bolshevik economy. Another possibility is a 'consolidation of power' question, which requires knowledge of a variety of topics — such as (in the case of Stalin) a good knowledge of both Stalin's use of terror and his use of propaganda and the arts to help him keep control.

The format of the topic questions in a typical examination paper is as follows:

Answer two questions from your chosen option.

You must answer Parts (i) and (ii) from your chosen questions.

Option 5: Russia 1903–1941

EITHER

1. (i) Explain how/why...
   (ii) To what extent was/did...?

OR

2. (i) Explain how/why...

(ii) '(Proposition)'. How far would you agree with this verdict?

OR

3. (i) Explain how/why...

(ii) '(Proposition)'. How far would you agree with this verdict?

OR

4. (i) Explain how/why...

(ii) To what extent was/did...?

In other words,

- Part (i) will require candidates to list a number of points (expanding on each one).
- Part (ii) requires candidates to give evidence in support of a proposition, but also to give evidence against the proposition.

Examinable skills

Sixty marks are available for Unit 2. Marks will be awarded for demonstrating the following skills:

- focusing on the requirements of the question
- showing a clear understanding of the past
- remembering, choosing and using historical knowledge
- explaining, analysing and making a judgement
- showing links between the key factors of your explanation

Focusing on the requirements of the question

Read the question carefully.

Part (i) of the question will always ask how or why something happened. Part (i) does not expect candidates to examine other factors. For example, if asked

Explain how the Bolsheviks used propaganda to consolidate their power in Russia between 1917 and 1924.

you are not required to consider other methods, such as force. Essentially, at least four or five points are expected, with evidence to support them.

Part (ii) will be 'To what extent...' or 'How far...' was something the case. A detailed examination of the proposition in the question is expected, followed by a careful consideration of the counter-argument. Therefore, in the question

To what extent was propaganda the most important factor in the Bolsheviks' consolidation of power between 1917 and 1924?

other factors, such as use of force, do need to be explored. Such balance in a question is essential for top-mark answers. As with Part (i), evidence is required to support points made.

Showing a clear understanding of the past

Your understanding of the past may be shown in a variety of ways. Detailed evidence can be used to show understanding. An explanation of which factors were the most important in causing a particular situation also proves you have a good understanding of the issues. A good, insightful introduction or conclusion also reveals that you have a clear grasp of what went on.

Remembering, choosing and using historical knowledge

Once you have worked out what the question requires, you have to choose the parts of your knowledge which are relevant. It is best — particularly for the 22-mark part of the question — to plan your knowledge in the order you intend it to appear in your essay.

The 8-mark response often requires about five points. However, it may be the case that more points than this are required — and it is not uncommon for a mark scheme to refer to seven or eight.

In the 22-mark response, there should be roughly five or six points in the proposition and at least three or four points in the counter-argument. However, this is certainly not a rigid rule. The crucial thing is that your 22-mark response should be balanced.

For both 8-mark and 22-mark responses, the points made need to be supported with evidence — in other words, **specific, detailed examples**. Relevant names, dates, statistics, organisations and events should be included, as well as the appropriate historical vocabulary. It should be remembered that twentieth-century Russian history is peppered with technical vocabulary. Russian words and acronyms will need to be well learnt.

Note that while irrelevance in responses is not penalised, it does waste much-needed time. Indirectly, therefore, it could cost marks.

Analysing, explaining and making a judgement

An outline of events which are not related to the question will not score well. In mark schemes, this is described as 'narrative' and is to be avoided. Instead, candidates are encouraged to link their response to the question regularly. This is credited as 'clear explanation'. It is good practice to make these links at the start or end of a paragraph.

Good analysis takes place when a candidate considers the importance of the issues that he or she is considering. It is, for example, an indication of a top-level answer if a candidate can show how one cause of an event was more important than another, or why one result of an event mattered more than something else.

Showing links between the key factors of your explanation

This is another indicator to examiners of a top-level candidate. Links between key factors can be shown by considering the relative importance of different factors, as a form of analysis. They can also be shown by demonstrating how factors are dependent on each other.

Assessment levels

Answers are normally marked according to four assessment levels. The requirements for each level are shown below.

8-mark questions	22-mark questions
Level 1 (0–2 marks)	**Level 1 (0–5 marks)**
Inaccurate, with no detail Does not do what is asked for at all General and very unclear Poor standard of English	Very limited, with no detailed knowledge Poor understanding Too general and possibly narrative May be mostly irrelevant Defects in organisation Lacks specialist vocabulary
Level 2 (3–4 marks)	**Level 2 (6–11 marks)**
Frequently inaccurate, but some limited information given Starting to tackle the question Needs to be clearer Better English than for Level 1, but still a lot of mistakes	Less limited, but still very little detail Overall understanding shown Still quite general Making an attempt to do what the question asks for Occasional defects in organisation Little specialist vocabulary
Level 3 (5–6 marks)	**Level 3 (12–17 marks)**
Quite accurate, with more detailed information given Deals quite well with the question Reasonably clear and well laid out Sound standard of English	Quite good detail May have some gaps in knowledge and may have left something important out Specifically and clearly linked to the question Makes a judgement clearly related to the question Balanced (considering proposition and counter-argument) Good organisation Some specialist vocabulary
Level 4 (7–8 marks)	**Level 4 (18–22 marks)**
Extremely accurate and very detailed Totally focused on the demands of the question Extremely clear and very well laid out Very good standard of English	Very good detail Sustained evaluation Clearly linked to the question all the way through Showing good analysis of the question Very well balanced Very good organisation Appropriate use of specialist vocabulary

How to use this guide

Make sure you understand the layout of the examination paper, the pattern of marks and the types of question asked.

The **Content Guidance** section is structured specifically to enable you to tackle both 8-mark and 22-mark question parts. Make sure that you are clear on the concepts and vocabulary included in the guide. Be thoroughly familiar with individuals and organisations that are prominent during the period, and how they shaped events.

Use the **Questions and Answers** section to give you a clear idea of the standard expected for an A-grade answer. Also look carefully at the C-grade answers and note how flaws such as lack of detail, balance or focus can harm an answer and result in a lower mark.

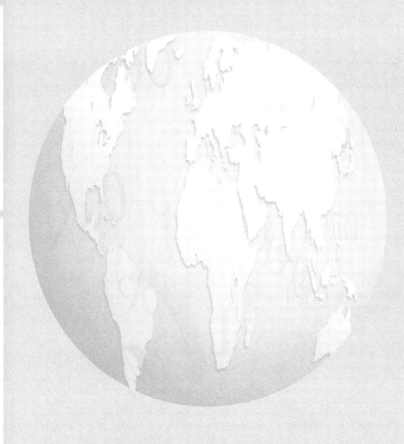

Content
Guidance

The specification for Russia 1903–41 states that the course covers three fundamental topics:

- Causes and consequences of the 1905 Revolution
- Lenin and revolution 1917–24
- Stalin and revolution 1924–41

This guide is designed to correspond as closely as possible to these fundamental topics. However, for the sake of clarity, the topic of 'Lenin and revolution' has been divided into:

- The 1917 revolutions
- Russia and the USSR under Lenin 1917–24

This option focuses on the history of Russia and the USSR from the later part of the reign of the last tsar, Nicholas II, through the revolutionary period of 1917 and the period of early Bolshevik control under Lenin, finishing with the rule of Stalin until the German invasion in 1941.

Understanding the causes and consequences of the 1905 Revolution is essential. You need to be aware of how the tsar strengthened his position until 1914, and of the fortunes of revolutionary groups that sought his downfall.

It is also necessary to understand the devastating impact of the First World War on the tsar's government, while grasping the reasons for his eventual downfall in February 1917. You need to appreciate why the Provisional Government that succeeded the tsar then collapsed, what was most important in bringing the success of the Bolshevik-led October Revolution, how the Bolsheviks overcame their rivals in the Civil War and how the one-party state was created.

An analysis of the Bolshevik economy will also be required, investigating how Bolshevik economic policy worked and how successful it was. It will also be necessary to grasp the cultural values of Lenin's Russia and how the Bolsheviks used propaganda and the arts to strengthen their regime.

Finally, you will need to understand how Stalin took over and controlled the USSR between 1924 and 1941. You will need to investigate the consistency and success of Stalin's economic policy, and his use of propaganda, culture and terror as methods of strengthening his control.

This guide will consider each of these fundamental topics in turn. However, examiners' questions may contain elements of more than one topic. For example, the causes of the February Revolution may be an 8-mark part in Question 2, while the causes of the October Revolution appear as a 22-mark part in Question 3.

Causes and consequences of the 1905 Revolution

Long-term problems faced by Russia at the turn of the twentieth century

In the early twentieth century, Russia faced a number of economic, social and political problems. Many of these contributed to the 1905 Revolution, and some contributed to the eventual downfall of the tsar.

Economic problems

The economic problems were serious. Russia suffered from a **backward agricultural system**. Strip farming meant that yields were low. The government imposed high taxes on peasants and took a considerable percentage of crops each year to export. These problems generated resentment among the peasants, which made many of them take part in the 1905 Revolution.

By 1914 Russian industry was growing rapidly, but this was from a very small base to start with. The economy was not strong enough to withstand the demands of a modern war.

Russia had a lot of **foreign debt**. Much of its industrial growth was funded by other European countries — particularly France — through loans. Thirty per cent of capital invested in Russia came from abroad. Any crisis in Europe therefore threatened Russia's financial stability.

To make matters worse, Russia fell into a period of **trade recession** at the turn of the century, which lasted until about 1906. This recession had its greatest impact on the poorest elements of Russian society — industrial workers and peasants. Harvests were poor, and workers and peasants were angry about unemployment and falling wages. Peasants also hated mortgage payments. All of this contributed to the 1905 Revolution.

Finally, and more generally, Russia was vastly bigger than any other country in the world. An extremely **inefficient transport network** made the country seem even more vast and inaccessible.

These problems would be highlighted and made worse by the Russo–Japanese War.

Social problems

The poorest in Russia suffered terribly at the turn of the twentieth century.

Industrial workers had to endure **terrible living and working conditions**. The tsar's government did very little to improve these. This made them more likely to turn to revolutionary political groups which claimed they could help them.

Many people were **illiterate**, and the majority of these were peasants. However, in a way this worked in the tsar's favour, because illiteracy blinded the peasantry to how miserable their lives were.

Apart from foreign loans, Russia's new industry was financed mainly through **tax**. Peasants were taxed heavily, even though they were least able to afford it.

All of this suffering was made worse by **continued repression**. In 1902 the novelist Leo Tolstoy, in an 'Open address to Nicholas II', described in detail the widespread denial of freedoms and political repression.

Political problems

Weaknesses in Russia's political system made it unlikely that the country's economic and social problems would be effectively dealt with.

There was an absence of representative institutions until 1906. Russia was an **autocracy**. One man (the tsar) made the final decision in all matters of government.

The last tsar of Russia, Nicholas II, was not a capable ruler. He was bored by paperwork and preferred to spend time with his family rather than attend to the everyday business of government. Nicholas was also determined not to change the autocratic system, believing that democracy would bring about the destruction of the Russian empire. The tsar's (and during the First World War the tsarina's) refusal to bring much-needed political change contributed both to the outbreak of the 1905 Revolution and to his downfall in February 1917.

Although a parliament (the **duma**) was established in 1906, the tsar largely ignored its recommendations. Furthermore, the **vote** was limited to the wealthiest people in society, and so those who sat in the duma usually reflected their conservative views. At local government level, demands for reform by the land assemblies (**zemstvos**) were nearly always ignored by the tsar and his government.

Government was highly **corrupt**. Those with powerful political contacts tended to be the ones who advanced, while promotion was rarely on merit. This led to incompetence and irresponsibility in government.

The Russian Orthodox Church was a major force against change. It had a big influence on the tsar.

All of these factors prevented the tsar from making changes that were badly needed.

Opposition to the tsar took three main forms (see page 19):
- **Liberal opposition.** After 1906 this was concentrated mainly in the duma and in the zemstvos. Liberals supported a strong role for parliament in running the country (which the tsar didn't allow) and insisted that the tsar stuck to Russia's constitution of October 1905 (which he would fail to do).
- **Revolutionary opposition.** At the start of the twentieth century the main revolutionary parties in Russia were the Socialist Revolutionaries and the Social Democrats (who in 1903 split into the Bolsheviks and the Mensheviks).
- **Opposition from non-Russian minorities.** About half of Russia's population wasn't ethnically Russian. The tsar's oppression often prompted both Jewish people (who suffered most) and members of other minorities to join revolutionary groups.

The situation before the 1905 Revolution

Witte, one of the tsar's most able ministers in the early twentieth century, remarked shortly before the 1905 Revolution that 'the world should be surprised that we have any government'. Given all the problems the tsar had, this was an understandable comment to make.

Causes of the 1905 Revolution

Economic causes

The tsar's government did very little to improve terrible living and working conditions. At the beginning of the twentieth century, Russia's industrial workers worked an average of 11 hours a day. Conditions in factories were very harsh, and little concern was shown for the health and safety of workers. This made them more likely to support the 1905 Revolution.

Witte contributed to many of Russia's agricultural problems, and a combination of heavy taxation and continuing exports of grain put real pressure on the peasants. This led to serious food shortages at the start of the century.

The period of trade recession put Russia's industrial workers in even more difficulty (see page 11).

The Russo–Japanese War of 1904–05

In the early years of the twentieth century Russia attempted to expand into Manchuria and Korea, but was opposed by Japan.

War broke out in February 1904, when the Japanese navy attacked the Russians at Port Arthur, eventually taking Port Arthur in January 1905. The Japanese also won important victories over Russia at Mukden (a land battle) and at Tsushima (a sea battle), where a large section of the Russian navy was destroyed.

Effects of the Russo–Japanese War

The war glaringly revealed the incompetence of the government. As a result, criticism of the government grew.

There was great discontent at home. **Bloody Sunday** was partly motivated by a desire to bring an end to the war. Moreover, Russia's defeat at the hands of a small Asian country was seen as a national humiliation.

Revolutionary activity increased. Defeat in the war by August 1905 was the trigger that led to a general strike and the formation of soviets, most famously in Saint Petersburg.

The war led to **shortages** and a rise in the rate of **inflation**. Inflation was already running at 20% in 1904, at the start of the war. The war made this problem worse.

Count Sergei Witte rose to prominence once more. He helped bring an end to the war with Japan, and as Prime Minister he introduced the **October Manifesto** (see pp. 15–16).

Eventually the war was officially ended with the Treaty of Portsmouth (New Hampshire, USA) in September 1905. This brought a settlement that was very favourable to Japan and ended Russian attempts to expand further into the Pacific.

Bloody Sunday, 1905

Causes

Russia's industrial workers suffered from very poor **working conditions** (for detail, see page 13).

Trade unions were not allowed. Factory owners refused to give in to workers' demands to have their own unions. As a result a priest called Father Gapon formed the Assembly of Russian Workers in 1903.

Inflation was rising. The Russo–Japanese war increased the rate.

Russian peasants feared that the government was about to seize their land if they had fallen behind in their 'redemption' (mortgage) payments to the government.

In January 1905 four members of the Assembly of Russian Workers were dismissed at the Putilov iron works. Gapon called for a **strike**, and 110,000 workers in Saint Petersburg took part.

Gapon then drew up a petition to give to the tsar, outlining workers' demands. In the **petition**, he asked for a range of social and political changes. These included:
- an 8-hour day for workers, increased wages, better working conditions and the right to organise in trade unions
- freedom of speech, press and religion
- universal suffrage
- an end to the Russo–Japanese War

Over 150,000 people signed the petition, and on 22 January 1905 Gapon led a large procession of workers to the Winter Palace to present the petition peacefully to Tsar

Nicholas II. They were attacked by police and Cossacks. Over 100 were killed and 300 wounded. This had been a demonstration by people loyal to the tsar. The response was greeted with dismay and anger. The event was known as 'Bloody Sunday'.

The events of the 1905 Revolution

Bloody Sunday was the event that triggered the 1905 Revolution. Strikes, disorder and terrorism spread out across the country. Former Prime Minister Plehve was assassinated by the Socialist Revolutionaries.

Large estates were attacked in the countryside, and the same happened to public buildings in the towns. Land and property were seized by peasants.

Georgia took advantage of the situation to declare itself independent. Jewish people demanded equal rights.

A 'Union of Unions' was set up in May 1905 by Pavel Milyukov, a leader of the Constitutional Democratic Party (known as the Kadets), with the aim of creating a broad-based alliance that would include peasants and factory workers. It declared the government to be a 'terrible menace'. However, it won little peasant support and was mainly middle-class in membership.

The Potemkin Mutiny broke out in June, when the sailors of the battleship *Potemkin* refused to obey orders and tried unsuccessfully to get the rest of the ships in their squadron to do the same. An attempt to raise support on land in the port of Odessa was crushed.

A soviet was set up in Saint Petersburg in the autumn. This was an attempt by revolutionaries to take control of the city. The soviet organised supplies and emergency measures. Trotsky was its chairman and organised several strikes in the city. A further 50 soviets sprang up across Russia.

Finally, a general strike took place in October 1905, organised by Trotsky. It was this event which did most to pressurise Nicholas II to pass the October Manifesto.

Results of the 1905 Revolution

Focus question

How far would you agree that tsarism was more secure after the 1905 Revolution than before it?

The October Manifesto and the dumas

Witte, recalled by Nicholas II in the summer of 1905, wrote the so-called October Manifesto. Effectively it was Russia's first constitution. In November the tsar went on to promise a reduction in mortgage repayments for peasants.

The October Manifesto included a range of promises from the tsar, such as:
- freedom of speech, assembly and worship
- trade unions to be made legal
- no imprisonment without trial

Furthermore, the October Manifesto made provision for the formation of a state duma. It was to be elected by universal male suffrage. No law could be passed without its consent. Crucially, however, the duma could not propose legislation.

While the dumas were responsible for some progressive laws, their power was heavily restricted. When their criticism went beyond what he was prepared to tolerate, the tsar simply closed them down. The first duma lasted only 73 days, and the second one only a few months. After this, property restrictions were placed on voters, and the duma became dominated by the wealthier classes.

At the same time as the opening of the first duma, the tsar issued his **Fundamental Laws**. In these he declared that 'supreme autocratic power' belonged to the tsar. Also, one of the duma's two houses of parliament would have most of its members appointed by the tsar. The duma's powers were thus restricted even more.

At the time, Nicholas told his mother he 'felt sick with shame at this betrayal of the dynasty'. Almost certainly he had little intention of keeping the promises made in the October Manifesto. Freedom of speech continued to be heavily regulated.

In fact, the October Manifesto still left the tsar with a significant amount of power. He retained the power of veto over the duma. In addition, the duma had no financial power — for example, it was not allowed control of the budget.

The Manifesto also allowed the tsar to keep control of the armed forces. By passing the Manifesto, Nicholas ensured the loyalty of the army's officer class, who could now be relied on to put down any remaining opposition.

The weakening of opposition to the tsar

The autocracy survived, without being significantly weakened. Trotsky commented that autocracy, 'although with a few broken ribs, had come out of the experience of 1905 alive and strong'.

The tsar's actions had a harmful effect on potential opposition. Nicholas II's reluctant promise of a duma divided liberals from socialists. Liberals saw the first duma as a significant advance, but moderate socialists urged a boycott of the first duma election. Later, the divided response of opposition parties to the closing down of the first duma left the Kadet Party scarcely able to recover.

Liberals were now wooed back to the tsar's side. Liberals had encouraged revolutionary activity as a way of putting the tsar under pressure to make necessary reforms. However, they didn't enjoy the experience of mixing with the workers during the revolution and backed out of it in the end, allowing the workers in Saint Petersburg to be crushed. Peter Struve, a former Marxist who joined the Kadets in

1905, spoke for many middle-class liberals when he said, 'Thank God for the tsar, who has saved us from the people.' There was thus little prospect of any future united action between liberals and workers.

Organised revolutionary groups played little part in the 1905 Revolution. With the exception of Trotsky, none of the Social Democrats (Bolsheviks or Mensheviks) made an impact on events.

Revolutionaries were not won over by the Manifesto. Trotsky rejected it as 'the police whip wrapped in the parchment of the constitution'. Revolutionary opposition to the tsar, however, remained limited and unable to capitalise on displays of discontent.

Lessons and warnings for the future

The tsar's image as 'Little Father' — the guardian of the Russian people — was badly damaged by Bloody Sunday. Although he largely escaped having to make significant concessions after the 1905 Revolution, this did not mean that there were not important lessons he needed to learn from it. However, he failed to learn them.

The 1905 Revolution provided a warning for the tsar and his government of **discontent in the countryside**. Urban workers were a suspected source of trouble, but generally, up to this point, peasants had been loyal to the tsar.

Additionally, for the first time, the tsar could be held to account for specific **promises** made. This made it harder for him to escape the blame for future problems.

While the tsar failed to learn the lessons of the 1905 Revolution, the same could not be said of the revolutionaries. They now had an **example** for 1917 in terms of timing, tactics and organisation. The soviets that were set up in a number of Russian cities in 1905 would be an example to the Bolsheviks in 1917 of how to control a country.

Stolypin, 1906–11

Stolypin was made Minister of the Interior in April 1906. In July 1906 he was made Prime Minister.

He was an outstanding government minister, with a clear, if unusual, view of how to keep the tsarist system secure. This involved a mixture of reform and repression.

Reform, and why

The most significant reforms Stolypin introduced were a series of **land reforms**. He wanted to improve Russian agriculture to feed the country's growing population.

Stolypin believed that the creation of a stable group of prosperous farmers could help stave off revolution by making Russian peasants into a conservative political force — **'de-revolutionising' the peasantry**. He realised how fragile the tsarist system was. He defined his policy as the **'wager on the strong'**. In other words,

Stolypin encouraged wealthier peasants to buy their own land, in the hope that they would become more loyal supporters of the tsar. He introduced a number of reforms aimed at helping peasants.

In 1906 the hated land captains were abolished and the peasant passport system was ended. Peasants were now able to move around as freely as any other Russian. Stolypin also released the peasants from their obligations under the **mir** (peasant commune). They could now choose their own land as individuals, rather than as part of the *mir*. The *mir* had been a centre of revolutionary activity, so removing peasants from it would, Stolypin hoped, make tsarism more secure. Stolypin believed the other benefit of this was that it enabled those who left the *mir* to move away from the inefficient 'strip system' of farming.

In 1907 Stolypin ended the requirement for peasants to make redemption payments to the government for their land. Many peasants simply could not afford these. Stolypin realised this had been one of the reasons why many of them had supported the 1905 Revolution. A special **Land Bank** was set up to provide funds for independent peasants to buy their own land. As well as this, a voluntary resettlement scheme was set up to populate Russia's eastern territories with newly independent peasants and turn these regions into food-growing areas.

One effect of the land reforms was better relations with the duma, which was very cooperative in helping Stolypin to carry them through.

In addition to his land reforms, Stolypin introduced other progressive pieces of legislation. He gave people in rural areas more freedom to select who would represent them in the land assemblies (zemstvos). Meanwhile his Health Insurance Act of 1907 was one of the few attempts made to improve conditions for Russia's industrial workers.

Did Stolypin's land reforms work?

On the face of it, Stolypin's land reforms did make sense. There was indeed a group of strong peasant farmers who had the potential to be open to change. However, the problem was that there were not enough reforms to bring the modernisation of agriculture that Stolypin desired. Stolypin himself said the 'wager on the strong' needed 20 years to have a chance of working.

Few major changes came into Russian agriculture. In 1914 the strip system of farming was still widespread and only about 10% of the land had been consolidated into farms — most peasants preferred to live in the communes.

However, Stolypin's land reforms did create concern among revolutionary leaders. Just before the First World War, Lenin expressed his concern that Stolypin's reforms might have succeeded in weakening revolutionary activity.

Repression

Despite the significant number of reforms carried out by Stolypin during his time as prime minister, he was known more for repression than for reform.

In 1906 he declared a policy of **martial law**. As part of this he introduced a new court system (including new courts martial) that made it easier to arrest and convict political revolutionaries. Over 2,500 suspects were executed by these special courts between 1906 and 1911. As a result of this action, the hangman's noose in Russia became known as 'Stolypin's necktie'.

Furthermore, in 1907 Stolypin brought in a new electoral law which allowed only the wealthy to vote, therefore ensuring a conservative majority in the third duma.

On 1 September 1911 Stolypin was murdered by a member of the Socialist Revolutionaries. Opinion has varied about whether or not his death was the decisive blow to the chances of the tsarist system surviving.

The growth of opposition

Liberal opposition

Until the October Manifesto was issued, political parties had been illegal in Russia, although they were still formed. The main two liberal parties after 1905 were the Kadets (Constitutional Democrats) and the Octobrists (supporters of the October Manifesto).

The Kadets
The Kadets wanted a constitutional monarchy in which the powers of the tsar would be restricted by a democratically elected parliament. They were broadly middle-class in membership. Their leader was Milyukov. Many had taken part in the zemstvos and supported an easing of the situation for Russia's peasants.

The Octobrists
The Octobrists called themselves this because of their support for the October Manifesto. They were mainly businessmen (such as Guchkov) and landowners (such as Radzianko). Both men would take part in the Provisional Government of 1917. The Octobrists were broadly loyal to the tsar and supported the Russian empire. However, they were prepared to criticise the short-sightedness or incompetence of the tsar's government.

Revolutionary opposition

The Socialist Revolutionaries
The Socialist Revolutionaries (or Socialist Revolutionary Party, known as the SRs) were the most popular revolutionary group, and remained that way right up to the Bolshevik Revolution of 1917.

They employed a strange combination of tactics. On the one hand, they were in favour of open terrorist activity (although some favoured a more traditionally Marxist approach which was less dedicated to terrorism). On the other hand, however, they took part in the second duma. Later, they would also participate in the soviets and the Provisional Government of 1917.

The Socialist Revolutionaries suffered from being easily infiltrated by secret police (**Okhrana**) spies, such as Azef, the deputy leader and the man who masterminded Plehve's assassination. The SR who killed Stolypin was also an *Okhrana* spy.

The Social Democrats (Bolsheviks and Mensheviks)

Until 1903, the Bolsheviks and Mensheviks were members of a single political party, the Social Democrats or Social Democratic Party. However, after a disagreement on strategy in 1903, the Social Democrats split into two groups: the Bolsheviks (the name being derived from the Russian word for 'majority') and the Mensheviks (from the word for 'minority'). There were a number of reasons for the split.

One major difference between the Bolsheviks and Mensheviks concerned party structure. Lenin wanted to force members of the party to choose between Plekhanov's idea of a broad-based party and his own concept of a small, tightly knit and exclusive party.

There were differences over party organisation. The Bolsheviks believed in **'democratic centralism'** — in other words, that authority within the party should be held by the Central Committee of the party. Actually, it wasn't very democratic at all. This ran against the Menshevik view that there should be open, democratic discussion within the party.

There were also differences over the timing of the revolution. The Mensheviks believed Russia was not yet ready for proletarian revolution. Lenin's view was that the bourgeois and proletarian stages could be 'telescoped' into one revolution in a short time.

Finally, there were differences over tactics. The Bolsheviks opposed the Menshevik strategy of cooperating with other political parties and supporting trade unions by pursuing better wages and conditions for workers. Lenin believed that the only way workers could be transformed into a revolutionary force to overthrow capitalism was by letting conditions worsen. The resulting bitterness would drive workers on to revolt.

Who were the Bolsheviks and the Mensheviks?

The Bolsheviks

Lenin was the Bolshevik leader. Until 1917, many Bolsheviks spent long periods in exile, including Lenin himself. As a result, the Bolsheviks organised training schools abroad to train revolutionaries who would then return to Russia to infiltrate workers' organisations such as trade unions.

They funded themselves through **acts of crime**, such as robberies. This was how the young Stalin contributed to the Bolshevik cause early on. This contrasted with the Mensheviks' broadly legal methods.

The Bolsheviks were **not** considered to be **a serious threat** to the tsarist system — the police did not even list them as a major challenge. Before 1914 they numbered only between 5,000 and 10,000.

The Mensheviks

The main Menshevik leaders at the start were Plekhanov, Martov and Trotsky. Like most revolutionary parties, they had a cautious attitude to the 1905 Revolution. Plekhanov was an unenthusiastic supporter (although Trotsky was much more heavily involved). **Internal divisions**, due in part to their openness, weakened the Mensheviks.

The Mensheviks were less disciplined than the Bolsheviks. This was partly because the Mensheviks wanted to involve everyone who wished to support their revolution. (In contrast, the Bolsheviks believed any revolution should be guided by a small, well-organised elite.) It was also partly because the Mensheviks were more open than the Bolsheviks, which made the Mensheviks more **popular** until 1917.

They supported democracy. Plekhanov worried that Lenin would use the Bolshevik Central Committee to set up a dictatorship in Russia. The country would be swapping one form of authoritarian government for another.

Plekhanov and other Mensheviks opposed the Bolsheviks' views on the timing of a Marxist Revolution. They believed it was necessary to wait until after capitalism controlled Russia. The Mensheviks were therefore more inclined to go into coalition with democratic parties.

Opposition from non-Russian minorities

As shown earlier, the persecution of ethnic minorities in Russia meant they were more likely to support revolutionary groups.

Russification

The government strictly enforced a policy of restricting the influence of the non-Russian national minorities within the empire by emphasising the superiority of all things Russian.

Discrimination against non-Russians became open and vindictive in the 1890s. This was especially the case with Jewish people. Government interference in their education, religion and culture became widespread and systematic.

Anti-Semitism

There were 5 million Jews in Russia at the turn of the century. Nicholas II allowed **pogroms** to take place against Jews in the areas where they lived. These attacks resulted in the widespread killing of Jewish people and destruction of their property. During Nicholas II's reign, the number of pogroms increased sharply.

The Bund

Many Jews responded to the persecution by joining revolutionary movements. Jewish men such as Martov and Trotsky, for example, became Mensheviks.

In 1897 Jews formed their own revolutionary 'Bund' or union. Its aim was to unite Jewish communities across the Russian empire. It worked mainly as a trade union, but also as a political party. The Bund was active during the 1905 Revolution. It was also one of the influences behind the formation of the Social Democrats in 1898.

Russia, 1911–14

Focus question

To what extent was the Russian empire secure on the eve of the First World War?

Problems

The tsar faced serious difficulties between 1911 and 1914. The death of Stolypin in 1911 was a big blow to the tsarist regime's prospects of survival. Stolypin was a Prime Minister of great ability. None of his successors had the ability or the individual initiative to introduce the changes needed to guarantee the regime's survival. For example, Ivan Goremykin, Prime Minister in 1914, was 74 and almost certainly appointed to prevent further reforms.

There is also some reason to doubt whether Stolypin's policies had really worked. His reforms resulted in only 10% of peasants living outside the potentially revolutionary peasant commune.

The **Lena goldfields incident** of 1912 once again exposed the brutality of the tsar's government. Gold miners in the Lena region of Siberia demanded better pay and conditions. Troops fired on the miners, killing or injuring many. This reopened the whole issue of workers' rights. An *Okhrana* report in 1912 referred to this as a major reason for hostility towards the government at this time.

Despite this, however, the Lena workers focused on working conditions rather than on overthrowing the tsar. Also, revolutionaries proved to be unable to capitalise on this and other spells of discontent after 1906.

Significant **opposition** to the tsar had developed in the duma. Compared with the first and second dumas, the fourth duma (1912–17) was conservative, but it was prepared to be critical of the government. In 1913, the duma expressed its concern about the refusal of the government to pay attention to public opinion. This duma became a centre of opposition to the tsar during the First World War. It was partly duma representatives who helped persuade the tsar to abdicate in February 1917.

There were also worrying **economic problems**. Industrial growth lagged behind that of western countries. Russia's industrial growth was significant between 1906 and 1914, but in 1914 it was still producing less steel than its main competitors, Germany, the USA, Britain and France.

Agriculture remained **weak**. Stolypin's reforms took no account of the rising rural population. On the eve of the war, agricultural yields remained largely unchanged, at about half those of western Europe. Bumper harvests between 1909 and 1913 blurred the weaknesses of the landholding system.

Positive signs

It would be too easy, however, to accept that the downfall of the tsar and his regime was inevitable before the First World War.

The **return of the troops** after the war with Japan helped the tsar. These loyal troops gave the tsar more security and helped him keep control over potential unrest.

There were signs that the tsar still enjoyed considerable **popularity**. The 300th anniversary of the Romanov dynasty in 1913 was well supported. This suggests that there was still strong support for the tsar and the tsarist system. The tsar was still not seen by most peasants as responsible for the failures of his government.

Until the First World War, the tsar retained the grudging support of the middle class. After the 1905 Revolution, the possibility of a workers' revolution was their greatest fear. However, some historians believe that given the hostility of the tsar to change, conflict with the middle classes was bound to happen eventually.

Trade unions were weak and getting weaker after Stolypin's period as prime minister. Trade union membership dropped from 300,000 in 1907 to 40,000 in 1913. Strike action declined steadily as well.

Revolutionary groups were also weak. Revolutionaries had been caught unawares by the 1905 Revolution, and had been unable to harness it. They were weaker still in 1914. Lenin and Trotsky (both in Austria), along with a number of other Bolshevik and Menshevik leaders, were in exile when war broke out in August 1914. In 1910 one group of Bolsheviks wrote in their newspaper *Vpered* ('Forward') of their concern that their organisations were shrinking and that many local groups had disintegrated altogether as a result of arrests and banishments.

There were also divisions among and within revolutionary groups. Although the Bolsheviks and Mensheviks still shared the name 'Social Democrats', they were very clearly divided over methods. Mensheviks favoured the legal approach and were collaborating with moderate parties, unlike the Bolsheviks.

The Socialist Revolutionaries struggled to appeal to peasants and were weakened by infiltration by *Okhrana* spies. Meanwhile, Lenin expressed his concern that Stolypin's reforms might be succeeding in weakening the revolutionaries, as has been detailed earlier.

Furthermore, while Russia had serious structural weaknesses in its economy, it experienced an **economic recovery** between 1906 and 1914. Production in many key areas rose significantly. For example, in 1900 coal production was 16.1 million tonnes, but in 1913 it was 35.4 million tonnes.

There is thus much evidence to suggest that the tsar had every chance of survival in 1914, so long as he was prepared to make the political and economic adjustments needed for a modern state and could avoid any further catastrophic mistakes. Unfortunately, however, in August 1914 he made his biggest mistake of all — by entering the First World War.

The 1917 Revolutions

Focus questions

- Why did the February Revolution take place/the tsar fall from power?
- How important were short-term (First World War) and long-term causes of the downfall of Nicholas II?

Long-term causes of the downfall of Nicholas II

As we have seen, there were a number of long-term factors that contributed to the downfall of the tsar.

Economically, Russia was a huge country with serious weakness in its transport and agricultural systems and only a small industrial base. In the early twentieth century, it didn't possess a modern industrial economy and often struggled to provide for the needs of its people.

Politically, it had an inadequate ruler presiding over a corrupt and very unfair political system which he did his best to preserve.

The outbreak of the First World War highlighted these serious political and economic problems. In fact, it made them worse — to the point where the tsar could no longer remain on the throne.

The impact of the First World War and causes of the February Revolution

Political effects of the war/political reasons for the tsar's downfall

In 1915 the tsar took personal command of the army. This meant that his wife the **tsarina** had to take personal control of all domestic policy. She proceeded to rule very unsuccessfully, and her takeover of the government did great damage to the popularity of the royal family.

There was no consistency about the appointment of **ministers**. Thirty-six different government ministers served between 1915 and 1917. This in turn brought inconsistency to government policy.

Worse still, the tsarina placed an unhealthy amount of trust in the ex-monk **Rasputin**. Despite living an immoral and degenerate life in Petrograd (formerly

Saint Petersburg) before and during the First World War, Rasputin had a strong influence on government policy during the tsarina's time in charge, particularly over appointments to government. He was also highly corrupt.

However, there were other reasons why the tsarina made the royal family unpopular. She was German and was suspected of having pro-German sympathies. Rasputin and the tsarina were suspected of being German agents. Public faith in the tsarina's government was further weakened by her appointment of Boris Stürmer as Prime Minister in February 1916 — a man widely rumoured to be pro-German.

The tsarina also proved just as determined as the tsar to preserve the autocratic system. The royal family's contempt for the duma contributed to their downfall, as the dismissal of the fourth duma at the beginning of 1917 was one of the grievances which brought the outbreak of the February Revolution.

There was **mounting duma opposition** to the tsar and the tsarina. In August 1914 the duma had shown its support for the tsar by voting to dissolve itself until the war was over. However, after crushing military defeats in 1914, it demanded to be recalled — and in July 1915 it was.

Zemgor, a joint organisation of zemstvos and municipal councils, highlighted the government's failures and hinted that there might be a workable alternative to the tsarist system.

After the duma was recalled, a **'Progressive Bloc'** was formed there, made up of Kadets, Octobrists, Nationalists and some industrialists. The bloc, which mainly objected to the way the war was being run, was ignored by the tsar.

As pressure on the tsar grew in early 1917, it was army leaders and duma representatives rather than revolutionaries or workers who persuaded him to abdicate. It was thus the people whose support he only just kept in 1905 who helped end the tsar's rule.

Economic effects of the war/economic reasons for the tsar's downfall

During the First World War, Russia's fragile economy collapsed dramatically. The country was not ready for the demands of a modern, industrial war. It had only 3.5 million industrial workers out of a population of 115 million in 1914. It was incapable of producing the large amounts of goods required for wartime, such as shells, weapons and uniforms. Its agricultural and transport systems were badly out of date.

Government policy did not help either. It failed to coordinate food, fuel and transport resources. The situation was made worse by the poor relationship between the government, the duma and the zemstvos.

During the war, **industrial output** dropped by 50% between 1914 and the start of 1917. The main problems here were the conscription of industrial workers for the war and their replacement by untrained peasants.

As a result, **inflation** increased rapidly — by 400% between 1914 and 1917. For certain crucial food crops such as wheat and potatoes, the price rises were even sharper.

Industrial workers' wages could not keep up with the rising prices. This was one of the grievances that triggered the February Revolution, and was demonstrated at the Putilov steel works strike in Petrograd.

Agriculture was also hit hard by the war. Shortages grew worse, particularly for industrial workers. The area of land under cultivation fell by 20% in the First World War, as peasants were conscripted into the army and horses were seized for army use. Priority in **food** supply went to the army rather than to workers. Furthermore, a poor transport system prevented food reaching the cities — often it was left rotting in railway stations.

Worker discontent over food shortages was a major contributor to the downfall of the tsar, for example causing the discontent on International Women's Day, a trigger event for the February Revolution.

Military effects of the war/military reasons for the tsar's downfall

Russia was always very likely to suffer militarily during the First World War, because it was not prepared for the demands of a total war. Its officers were poorly trained. Soldiers had out-of-date weapons. Only one in three had a rifle. Some had no boots. Communications were poor.

The military situation weakened the tsar in a number of ways.

Russia suffered what were easily the highest **casualties** of any country in the war. It lost 8 million killed, wounded or captured.

Nicholas badly damaged the stability of his regime by deciding to take over command of the army in 1915. This did not improve the army's fortunes against the Germans. In fact, after he took command, more than 1 million were killed in defeats in Galicia and elsewhere in Poland. All this punctured the myth that the tsar was not responsible for his country's failures.

Defeats at the front sapped **morale** in the army and at home. Although this had little to do with the causes of the February Revolution, it was important for the outbreak of the October Revolution. The Bolsheviks infiltrated the army and used the defeats to encourage mutiny.

In addition, the demands of war meant the army could no longer be used as a security force at home.

Nevertheless, there is a danger of overstating military factors as a reason for the tsar's downfall. In 1916 the Russian army staged a recovery, with victories over the Austrians during the Brusilov offensive, which Michael Lynch in *Reaction and Revolution: Russia 1894–1924* (Hodder) believes brought the Austrians close to total collapse.

Events of the February Revolution

In February 1917, the February Revolution took place. It was essentially a spontaneous explosion of anger against economic problems (such as food shortages and low wages) and political problems (such as the closure of the fourth duma).

By the end of February, Nicholas had been forced out of power. He made an attempt to return to Petrograd to restore order, but was intercepted at Pskov, where a delegation of army and Duma leaders persuaded him to abdicate. Attempts to install his brother, Grand Duke Michael, on the throne failed.

Most prominent in the February Revolution were the **industrial workers**, rather than the middle classes or even the revolutionary groups (many of whose members were still in exile). There had been growing opposition to the tsar from workers for some time. By the start of 1917 there were 1,330 strikes, including most famously the one at the Putilov steel works, one trigger of the February Revolution.

A **Provisional Government** was then set up. Although it was mostly middle class and liberal, it also included Socialist Revolutionaries and Mensheviks.

Most of those who formed the Provisional Government had little to do with the February Revolution. Some had been excluded from the influential court circle. Others were frustrated at having been ignored when they tried to argue their case in the duma. From the outset, therefore, the Provisional Government was not in touch with the essential needs of the Russian people.

The Petrograd Soviet and the problem of dual authority

At the same time as the establishment of the Provisional Government, soviets were springing up all over the country, the most powerful one being in Petrograd. The Provisional Government and the **Petrograd Soviet** largely shared power. This meant that the Petrograd Soviet was an alternative source of authority to the Provisional Government. This would weaken the Provisional Government significantly.

At first, broadly speaking, the Provisional Government and the Petrograd Soviet did not clash with each other. However, there was one exception. In March 1917 the Petrograd Soviet issued Order Number 1. This weakened the Provisional Government by instructing that in the event of a conflict between the Provisional Government and the Petrograd Soviet, soldiers should obey the soviet rather than their officers. This meant that the soviets, rather than the Provisional Government, had real control of the army.

As time wore on, the soviets challenged the authority of the Provisional Government more and more. This was because they were elected, unlike the Provisional

Government. It was also because they took control at local level. In some places they became responsible for a number of vital everyday services, such as food supplies and the post and telegraph services.

The October Revolution

The October Revolution took place in October 1917. The Bolshevik Red Guards took over the headquarters of the Provisional Government in Petrograd, and a week later the Bolsheviks took control of Moscow.

In the event, the Bolshevik revolution was almost bloodless. Bolsheviks seized control of an almost deserted Winter Palace, defended only by a detachment of Cossacks and a women's battalion.

Reasons for the success of the October Revolution

Lenin's role and influence

Before Lenin returned from exile in April 1917, the Bolsheviks were very disorganised. Under him they regrouped. Lenin made a number of important contributions to the Bolsheviks' success.

Immediately upon his return to Russia, Lenin announced his **April Theses**, in which he demanded the handing over of 'all power to the soviets' and an immediate withdrawal from the war. According to Chris Corin and Terry Fiehn in *Communist Russia under Lenin and Stalin*, this brought the Bolsheviks support and made them the only true opposition to the Provisional Government. No other party had a political programme. The *April Theses* therefore gave the Bolsheviks a clear focus that other parties lacked.

Lenin gave the Bolsheviks a sense of urgency. He pressurised the Central Committee into staging a revolution as soon as possible. In winning them over, he had to overcome significant opposition from prominent leaders such as Kamenev and Zinoviev.

Lenin insisted on taking **control of the soviets**. He realised that increasingly in 1917 the soviets were the real government of Russia rather than the Provisional Government. Partly thanks to his determination, the Bolsheviks had taken control of the Moscow and Petrograd Soviets by the end of September.

Lenin had a ruthless ability to **exploit the mistakes** of the Provisional Government. The government decided to continue with the First World War. Lenin's slogan (which he stole from the SRs), 'Bread, Peace, Land', exploited the failure of this policy, as well as the policy of delaying land reforms until after elections. He also exploited other mistakes, such as the decision of Minister for Justice Kerensky to allow freedom of the press. Lenin made the most of this by savagely attacking the Provisional Government in the Bolshevik newspaper *Pravda*.

Lenin urged **non-cooperation** with the Provisional Government. This strategy ran against that of other Bolsheviks such as Stalin and Kamenev. However, it proved to be an extremely clever move. The Bolsheviks, unlike other revolutionary parties, now could not be associated with Provisional Government mistakes.

However, Lenin did make one important mistake which set back the Bolsheviks. He was unable to prevent the Bolsheviks from taking part in the unsuccessful July Days uprising. This resulted in a brief return to exile for Lenin and the arrest of key Bolshevik leaders.

The role of Trotsky

While Lenin was the great influence behind the October Revolution, it was Trotsky who actually organised it. Stalin wrote of Trotsky in 1918, 'All the practical work in connection with the organisation of the uprising was done under the immediate direction of Comrade Trotsky.'

Trotsky (unlike Lenin) was well known after his role in the 1905 Revolution. This experience helped the Bolshevik movement.

Trotsky was important in making sure the timing of the revolution was right, persuading Lenin to wait until October to make sure the Bolsheviks were strong enough to go ahead.

The key to Trotsky's success was his election as **chairman of the Petrograd Soviet** in September 1917. Under the Petrograd Soviet's authority was the Bolshevik-controlled organisation which actually carried out the October Revolution, the Military Revolutionary Committee (MRC). One of its three leaders was Trotsky, who commanded the Red Guard. They were the only effective military or even legitimate force in Petrograd.

Trotsky, within the MRC, drafted plans for the overthrow of the Provisional Government. When Lenin gave the order for the uprising to begin, it was Trotsky who directed the Red Guards in their seizure of the key vantage points in Petrograd.

Trotsky made a number of other key contributions to the success of the October Revolution. He added to the popularity of the Bolsheviks through his **speech-making**. He was able to exploit popular issues, accusing the Provisional Government of encouraging 'the bony hand of hunger'.

Partly thanks to Trotsky's popularity, Bolshevik appeal rose noticeably in 1917. In February 1917, the Bolsheviks had only 25,000 members. By October, there were almost 350,000. By then, the Bolsheviks were more popular than the Mensheviks.

However, it is important not to overstate Trotsky's contribution. Trotsky did not return to Russia from exile until May 1917, by which time Lenin had already issued his *April Theses*. He did not even join the Bolsheviks until that summer, having originally been a Menshevik.

The emergence of soviets across the country

Both Lenin (who insisted on their takeover) and Trotsky (as chairman of the Petrograd Soviet) were important in helping the Bolsheviks to take over the soviets.

Although at first they did little to clash with the Provisional Government, by the time the Bolsheviks had taken control of them the soviets were much more revolutionary than the Saint Petersburg Soviet of 1905 had been. These elected soviets made a much stronger claim to the people's loyalty than the Provisional Government did.

The process of taking over the soviets was made easier for the Bolsheviks because they were the only party to attend them regularly throughout the year of 1917, despite not being the largest party in them.

By now, the soviets had responsibility for much of the day-to-day business of running Russia. Thus when the Bolsheviks stormed the Winter Palace, the headquarters of the Provisional Government, in October 1917, they were practically running the country already.

Weaknesses of the Provisional Government

The Provisional Government was weak in a number of ways. The most obvious one was the fact that it was provisional, and therefore never meant to last. As it was unelected, it had no authority — in contrast to the Petrograd Soviet. It was further weakened by having to share power with the Petrograd Soviet (dual authority), which grew steadily more powerful as 1917 wore on.

Another difficulty was the fact that it was a coalition government with a variety of political views, ranging from conservative to revolutionary. As a result, it struggled to make laws, for fear of creating splits. Furthermore, it was reluctant to pass any major legislation until the war was over and elections could be held.

Mistakes of the Provisional Government

While in many ways the Provisional Government was unfortunate to be in the position it was, it did contribute greatly to its own downfall.

- It failed to introduce land reforms or elections. This helped to boost Bolshevik popularity, as Lenin exploited the Provisional Government's failure here by promising to put it right, using the slogan 'Bread, Peace, Land'.
- Kerensky, as Minister for Justice, made an early miscalculation in deciding to disband the *Okhrana*, which had been so helpful to the tsar in restricting revolutionary parties before the war. The Provisional Government also permitted **freedom of the press** — another key mistake (see page 28).
- The Provisional Government's decision to continue the **war** was a disaster. Whether it had much choice in the matter is debatable, however, given that Russia in 1917 was bankrupt and needed to keep fighting to secure war credits from its allies.
- The Russian army was torn apart after the decision of Kerensky (as Minister for War) to launch the June offensive in Galicia. This serious military defeat led to the July Days uprising. It also had other serious results. Demoralised soldiers retreated over a huge area. Disillusioned soldiers deserted in large numbers to claim their share of the land that was dramatically seized from the landlords after the Provisional Government's failure to introduce land reforms.
- **Desertions** across the army now became so widespread that by the time of the October Revolution the Winter Palace was practically undefended. All of this ultimately stemmed from the decision to continue the war.

- At home, it became easier to doubt the concern of the Provisional Government for the ordinary Russian. Government repression in the spring, summer and autumn of 1917 damaged the reputation of socialists within the Provisional Government (such as Kerensky, War Minister and, after July, Prime Minister) with Russian workers and peasants. Strict measures were taken against peasant land seizures, and the July Days uprising was put down ruthlessly. The socialists were discredited by the Bolsheviks for compromising with the 'bourgeoisie'.
- Possibly the Provisional Government's biggest mistake of all was the way it handled the **Kornilov affair**. Once again, Kerensky was heavily involved. Kornilov, commander-in-chief of the army, made the decision in August 1917 to march on the capital Petrograd. He claimed he wished to prevent Russia from being overrun by a socialist-inspired insurrection. Kerensky was concerned that Kornilov really wished to seize power. After some initial hesitation, Kerensky called on the citizens of Petrograd to defend the city. This included the Bolsheviks, who found themselves presented with a chance to re-establish themselves after the July Days. Kerensky released the Bolshevik leaders from prison and even armed them. Ironically, these weapons would be used to attack the Winter Palace in October. The issue boosted the Bolsheviks' reputation as patriotic defenders of the capital, while it exposed the vulnerability of the Provisional Government.

Russia and the **USSR** under Lenin 1917–24

The Bolsheviks in power

Focus question

How important was the role of Lenin in helping the Bolsheviks to consolidate their power over Russia between 1917 and 1924?

The Bolsheviks in October 1917

The Bolsheviks saw the October Revolution as only the starting point in the process of making Russia a truly socialist state. For this to happen, opposition would have to be crushed, the people would have to be 'politicised' (made into socialists), and an industrial economy would need to be established.

Bolshevik political aims

The Bolsheviks wished to establish a socialist dictatorship as soon as they got into power. They believed dictatorship was necessary, as the Russian people were not yet ready to rule themselves. They needed to be educated and politicised. While the Bolsheviks did establish a dictatorship in 1917, it was not until 1922 that they managed to establish a one-party state.

Lenin wished to set up a soviet socialist republic, as declared in his *April Theses* in 1917. The **1918 Constitution** fulfilled this intention. In 1922 this became the Union of Soviet Socialist Republics, or **USSR**.

The Bolsheviks needed to destroy their opponents. There was much opposition to the Bolsheviks from outside the party. In the elections to the constituent assembly, the Bolsheviks were far from the most popular party in Russia. The Socialist Revolutionaries dominated the vote in the countryside and won 370 seats in the elections to the Bolsheviks' 175. The SRs deeply resented Lenin's closure of the constituent assembly in January 1918, as did liberal parties such as the Kadets and the Octobrists. The Mensheviks also opposed the Bolsheviks. There also was opposition from tsarists. All these groups — along with Russia's former First World War allies, who wished to bring Russia back into the war — came together as the **'Whites'** in the Russian Civil War.

Abroad, the Bolsheviks intended to encourage **world revolution**. Many Bolsheviks believed that the revolution in Russia would only be secure if the country had socialist neighbours. They hoped that victory in the Civil War of 1918–20 would encourage Russia's neighbours to become socialist.

More immediately, the Bolsheviks needed to end the disastrous war with Germany. This was achieved at a significant cost at the **Treaty of Brest-Litovsk** in March 1918.

At home, the Bolsheviks needed to extend their authority across Russia. With this aim in mind, a party bureaucracy was set up across much of the country by 1921. The **Central Committee of the Communist Party** (the new name for the Bolsheviks after 1922) was in place by 1922.

Political problems faced by the Bolsheviks 1917–24

The groups opposing the Bolsheviks had support from Russia's former First World War allies. Between 1918 and 1920, opposition groups fought as the **Whites** along with the western allies against the Bolsheviks in the Russian Civil War. It was only after the defeat of the Whites that Lenin was able to take firm steps against his opponents.

Further opposition to Lenin and his policies came in 1921, during the **Kronstadt Mutiny** and the **Tambov Peasants' Revolt** — both against the policy of war communism. Opposition from the Kronstadt sailors was particularly worrying, as they had supported the October Revolution.

Lenin faced opposition from within the **party** as well. The 'Left' of the party opposed the Treaty of Brest-Litovsk and also Lenin's New Economic Policy (NEP). The question of how long the NEP should last remained unresolved by Lenin's death. Many had serious reservations about the *Cheka*, Lenin's secret police. Also the Workers' Opposition movement was against the harshness of Lenin's war communism policy.

Lenin had more success in dealing with another problem: the issue of **nationalities**. In 1917 and 1918, a number of non-Russian nationalities took advantage of the unstable political situation and the Brest-Litovsk treaty to secure independence for their territories. These included Finland, the Ukraine and Georgia. During the Civil War, Lenin accepted the independence of the non-Russian regions, so long as they established themselves as socialist states. Finally, in 1922, Russia absorbed five of the recently lost states back into the USSR.

Early methods of strengthening power

Establishment of a dictatorship

The principle of **'dictatorship of the proletariat'** was applied at once. This meant a dictatorship to rule in the people's interests until they were ready to take power for themselves. As yet, Lenin did not believe that the Russian people were capable of doing this.

Dissolving the constituent assembly

In January 1918, in elections to the new constituent assembly, the Bolsheviks won only a quarter of the seats; the Socialist Revolutionaries were much more popular. Lenin therefore used Trotsky's Red Guards to close down this new parliament. Now opposition to the Bolsheviks was deprived of a voice.

Use of the secret police, the *Cheka*

The *Cheka* was modelled on the tsarist secret police, the *Okhrana* — except that it was more efficient. Its founder was Dzerzhinsky.

The purpose of the *Cheka* was, according to Lynch in *Reaction and Revolution*, to destroy opponents (real or potential) of the Bolshevik regime. It spread a network of terror across Russia. It showed its ruthlessness in July 1918, with the assassination of the ex-tsar and his family. Now opposition was deprived of a potential leader.

Non-Russian nationalities given independence

Lenin's hope was that the non-Russian nationalities, former citizens of the Russian empire, would carry out their own socialist revolutions.

In some cases, the Bolsheviks had little choice but to let them go. The Treaty of Brest-Litovsk forced Russia to give independence to areas such as the Ukraine and Finland. In fact, a number of areas had already proclaimed their independence from Russia in 1917. Also, in 1919, British and German intervention in the Baltic forced the

Bolsheviks to accept the independence of Lithuania, Estonia and Latvia. Most were later absorbed into the Soviet Union.

An end to the war

The Bolsheviks were desperate to end Russia's involvement in the First World War. However, the Treaty of Brest-Litovsk, which ended the war for Russia, forced it to make major sacrifices. One-third of European Russia was lost, including the vital wheat-producing area of the Ukraine. Forty-five million people were lost, and Russia was required to pay 3 billion roubles in reparations.

The treaty brought opposition from within the Bolshevik Party. The 'Left' of the party wished to continue the war and destroy imperial and capitalist Germany. Lenin and Trotsky (Foreign Commissar) persuaded them with difficulty that as the collapse of the German empire was inevitable anyway, continued conflict was not necessary.

The first Soviet constitution, July 1918

The first Soviet constitution was more a declaration of intent by the Bolsheviks than an enforcement of Bolshevik policy. Nevertheless, it gave some clear indications of their intentions for the future. The main terms were:
- Russia was to become a soviet socialist republic.
- Russia was proclaimed a classless society.
- There would be no private ownership of property — everything would be controlled and distributed by the state for the people's benefit.
- Elections would be based on a soviet system.
- Universal suffrage would be granted.

Other early actions of the Bolsheviks

The most significant other early action taken by the Bolsheviks was the **Decree on Land** in October 1917. This stated that land was to be confiscated from landlords and the church and distributed among the peasants. The Bolsheviks stated in this decree that it was the 'first duty of the government' to settle the land question.

Effectively what Lenin was doing was accepting the legality of the peasant land seizures in the summer of 1917. Lenin's Decree on Land helped him win over some peasant support.

In other important early steps, the Bolsheviks abolished all private property and private enterprise. The banks and the railways were **nationalised**. Lenin cancelled all **foreign debts**. Also, improvements were made to the chaotic **transport system**.

Nevertheless, despite the effectiveness of many of the measures taken by the Bolsheviks at this time, they still had many enemies. There was the continuing loyalty of many to the tsar. There was also resentment at the way the Bolsheviks had won and secured power — for instance, closing down the constituent assembly. It was clear that the Bolsheviks were going to have to face down this opposition and defeat it.

The Russian Civil War 1918–20

Background

The Russian Civil War was fought between the Bolsheviks (the Reds) and everyone who opposed them (the Whites).

There were others who remained neutral (including those known as the **'Greens'**). Both the Reds and the Whites competed with each other to win over this group.

The Civil War took place against a backdrop of economic desperation. For many peasants, political beliefs came second to providing food for their starving families, so the majority of the population had little interest in who won the conflict.

The Whites

The Whites were a group of very loosely linked forces, united only by their hatred of the Bolsheviks.

There were former tsarist officers, who hated the Treaty of Brest-Litovsk. These included most of the most prominent White commanders, such as Marshal Denikin, Marshal Kornilov and Admiral Kolchak. There were revolutionary groups who were hostile to the Bolsheviks, such as the Socialist Revolutionaries. There were constitutional politicians such as the Kadets, who bitterly opposed the closing of the constituent assembly. Finally, there were foreign troops.

The Whites' main power bases were far away from each other, which made coordination of the White military effort practically impossible.

Difficulties for the Reds

At first, the Bolsheviks faced a number of difficulties.

They were surrounded. The Red Army was flanked to the north by foreign troops representing Russia's former First World War allies. To the east were Admiral Kolchak and the Czech Legion. In the south was Marshal Denikin.

Russia's former First World War allies fought with the Whites. They wanted to get Russia back into the war, on their side. They also saw the new Bolshevik revolutionary regime as a threat. The French in particular were eager to recover money and supplies invested in Russia.

However, the scale and success of the foreign intervention was not impressive. The bulk of the foreign armies was in northern Russia. They numbered no more than 150,000 men. These soldiers were war-weary after the First World War. Meanwhile, their commanders were unable to agree on war aims.

The most successful White forces were the Czech Legion. The Czechs occupied a large number of towns beyond the Ural mountains along the Trans-Siberian railway line in the summer of 1918 and formed (with the Socialist Revolutionaries) a White power base in the city of Omsk. However, they were too isolated.

In addition, the Bolsheviks inherited huge economic problems due to the war and the Treaty of Brest-Litovsk. The loss of the key wheat-producing area of the Ukraine was a bitter blow and contributed to the bread ration going down to 50 grammes per person per day by March 1918. Meanwhile, by June 1918, the Petrograd workforce had shrunk by 60%.

Reasons why the Bolsheviks won the war

The role of Trotsky

Trotsky was commander of the Red Army and contributed to the Reds' victory in many ways.

Trotsky **organised** the Reds well. His military objectives were kept simple and clear: to keep the Whites from grouping large forces together in one place, and to keep his army well supplied. Furthermore, under him the Reds fought for a single, clear political goal: to defend the Bolshevik revolution.

Trotsky gave the Red Army an iron **discipline**. He took an army on the point of disintegration and made it into an effective fighting force. He brought back thousands of former tsarist officers to command and train army units. To prevent betrayal, he had their families held hostage.

He restored a hierarchical **structure** to the Red Army. Soldiers' committees and the election of officers were ended. Ranks and saluting were reintroduced. There was harsh punishment for disobedience. The death penalty was introduced for a variety of offences, such as disloyalty or desertion. Political commissars were appointed to each army unit and ensured they were 'politically correct' (according to Corin and Fiehn in *Communist Russia under Lenin and Stalin*).

This tight discipline did not eliminate desertions, but it did make sure those who stayed performed well.

Trotsky was a **dynamic leader**:
- He used his specially armoured train to travel to the front lines to encourage his men as well as to supply them, and he inspired them with his speeches and his **personal courage**. The Whites had no general able to match Trotsky's qualities as a leader.
- He made a number of **important tactical decisions**. One of the most important was not to surrender Petrograd when it was under threat. He appreciated the symbolic value of the city where the October Revolution had taken place and raced to defend it, eventually turning the Whites away.
- He used Red Army units as part of the **Red Terror policy**, which effectively prevented the majority of peasants from opposing the Reds.
- He made sure the Reds controlled the main industrial and administrative centres. This gave them **access to supplies** that the Whites could not obtain. The Whites then had to seek supplies from abroad, enabling Lenin to claim that, in Lynch's words, the Whites were 'in league with foreign interventionists'.

Trotsky had some weaknesses as a military leader. Corin and Fiehn point out that he never claimed to be a great military strategist and was content to leave the key decisions to others. However, as a coordinator of military operations in the Civil War, he was outstandingly successful.

The role of Lenin

Lenin played an important role in support of Trotsky in helping to bring about Red victory. He contributed to the Reds' victory in a number of ways.

Lenin had a strong **propaganda** appeal. He won the Reds popularity by representing them as patriotic defenders of Russia against foreign interference. Good use was made of picture propaganda in particular, which appealed to Russia's peasants, most of whom were illiterate. Russia's most prominent female Bolshevik, Alexandra Kollontai, also played a key propaganda role.

Lenin made ruthless use of the so-called 'Red Terror'. He saw **terror** as a crucial form of control (it included the murder of the royal family in July 1918). He used the *Cheka* and Red Army units to enforce it: they ransacked peasant villages on the pretext of searching for 'counter-revolutionaries', but often simply to steal grain. Although this terror caused deep resentment, it did have the effect of preventing neutrals from opposing the Bolsheviks.

Lenin's war communism policy ensured that the **Red Army was well supplied**. During the Red Terror, requisition squads provided the army with surplus food seized from peasants. According to Corin and Fiehn, Lenin's management of Russia during the war communism period was vital to the success of the Bolsheviks.

Lenin **supported Trotsky's decisions**. For example, he backed Trotsky in the reestablishment of a hierarchy for the Red Army and the use of former tsarist officers to command and train the troops. Lenin's support was important here, as there was serious opposition from within the party to the move — from Stalin, for instance.

Finally, Lenin did not challenge the attempts of non-Russians to gain independence. However, many non-Russians still either remained neutral in the Civil War or fought on the side of the Whites.

The failings and mistakes of the Whites

The Whites were geographically **divided**. They fought as separate detachments and were easily picked off. Even when they did consider cooperating, they were too scattered. This contrasted with the Reds, who were centred around the main western cities.

The Whites were also politically divided. These political divisions prevented cooperation between the different White armies. The foreign troops in the north were committed to democracy. Meanwhile Kolchak and Denikin were tsarists, whose views made cooperation with revolutionary opponents of the Bolsheviks impossible.

Kolchak was very suspicious of the SR government in Omsk. All this contrasted once again with the Reds, who were united under a single political goal.

The Whites were badly **outnumbered**. The White army never numbered more than a third of a million men. Thanks to forced conscription, the Red Army grew to 5 million.

The Whites were very **badly disciplined**. Denikin once said, 'I can do nothing with my army. I am glad when it carries out my combat orders.' In Omsk, White army uniforms were sold on the black market, and officers lived in brothels in a haze of cocaine and vodka. Again, this stood in sharp contrast to the discipline of the Reds.

The Whites made themselves **unpopular**. Their cooperation with foreign armies and use of foreign supplies angered many Russians, and was expertly exploited in Bolshevik propaganda. Furthermore, White brutality meant that they could not expose the Reds' cruel methods. For example, White Cossacks in the south raped and murdered whole villages of Jews.

Although the Red Terror often turned peasants against the Reds, the Whites behaved no better, and so were unable to represent themselves as the better alternative. The Whites seemed merely to represent a return to the way things were under the tsar. For example, Denikin made it clear that it was his intention to restore recently confiscated land to the landlords.

How were the Bolsheviks strengthened by the Civil War?

Trotsky's prominent role in the Reds' victory makes the case that he was the most important figure in the Bolsheviks' consolidation of power. Red victory made it more likely that the Bolsheviks would hold on to power, for a number of reasons:

- **The Civil War put the Bolsheviks in a stronger position to move against their enemies.** In 1921, for example, they were able to arrest 5,000 Mensheviks, and in 1922 Russia became a one-party state. This would not have been possible without the reality of power that victory against the Whites gave them.
- **The Civil War helped the party (the Communist Party after 1922) to grow and increased its central control.** Lynch estimates that one-third of all members of the Communist Party in 1927 had joined in the years 1917–20 and believes that the move towards centralisation became greater as the Civil War dragged on, with more power going to the Politburo in particular.
- **The Civil War made the Bolsheviks tougher.** It gave them (according to Robert Tucker, quoted in Lynch, *Reaction and Revolution*) a greater 'readiness to resort to coercion', without which it is unlikely that they would have been able to keep control in these difficult years.

Economic policy

Focus questions

- How successful was the Bolsheviks' economic policy in 1917–24?
- How consistent was Bolshevik economic policy in 1917–24?
- To what extent did the Bolsheviks' economic policy help them to control Russia?

Bolshevik economic aims

- Lenin was committed to **centralisation** and **total state ownership** of industry and agriculture. State ownership of the economy was a genuinely socialist principle. A number of actions were taken to achieve this. For example, private property was abolished in November 1917. Later, a Decree of Nationalisation was issued in June 1918, to enable the state to take over all factories of more than ten workers.
- The Bolsheviks saw it as essential to **win the class war**. For Lenin, the struggle to establish a socialist economy was an 'internal front' in the fight against capitalism and imperialism that was going on in the Civil War.
- On a more practical level, Lenin needed to **improve production**. The Treaty of Brest-Litovsk limited Russia's agricultural capacity. Meanwhile, in the cities, Russia's industrial workers, who had seized the factories in 1917, proved incapable of running them. During the Civil War, the failure of agriculture caused a famine in which 5 million starved. Industrial production was hit at this time too, and the Petrograd workforce dropped drastically. However, the **New Economic Policy (NEP)** brought a relative improvement in production.
- The Bolsheviks wanted to instil a form of discipline in the workers and peasants similar to that which existed in the Red Army. Trotsky called this the **'militarisation of labour'**.
- Lenin needed to **end the inflation problems** that Russia had suffered during and after the First World War. Inflation became an even bigger problem during the Civil War, with the value of the rouble dropping in 1920 to 1% of its worth in 1913. Peasants could not be paid in paper money and so were unable to supply the industrial cities. Eventually the Bolsheviks had to establish a new currency as part of the NEP.
- The Bolsheviks aimed to make Russia a modern industrial nation with a **centrally controlled economy**. For example, electrification was one of the key targets of the NEP.
- Within the party there were significant differences in economic aims. The war communism policy came to be opposed by the 'Workers' Opposition', who saw it as too strict. The NEP was opposed by Trotsky and the 'Left' communists. However, **Bukharin**, the Bolsheviks' economic expert, saw the NEP as necessary in the circumstances.

Bolshevik economic problems

- The Bolsheviks struggled against **poor production rates**. During the First World War, industrial production had dropped by 50%. At the same time, inflation had increased by 400%. As already noted, this inflation worsened dramatically after 1918.
- Russia remained economically **backward**. It had a limited industrial base and a backward agricultural system. Agriculture was almost entirely non-mechanised. The war communism period made agriculture's problems even worse, with the 1921 grain harvest only 46% of the 1913 total.
- The **Treaty of Brest-Litovsk** added to Russia's economic difficulties. Russia was stripped of the Ukraine, its major wheat-producing area. Worse still, it had to pay a total of 3 billion roubles in reparations.
- **Production** rates dropped drastically during the war communism period, with iron production at less than 5% of its prewar levels.
- Finally, there were significant **divisions** over economic policy during Lenin's rule, which caused further problems. For example, the NEP was criticised by many in the party who had welcomed the strict measures under war communism.

The different economic policies

State capitalism, 1917–18

During 1917–18, Lenin followed a policy of state capitalism. Essentially this meant that the Bolshevik government would continue to use the existing economic structures until a fully-fledged socialist system could be adopted.

The economic measures that were taken were designed mainly to confirm actions that had already taken place. These included the Decree on Land (October 1917), which made legal the peasant land seizures of the summer of 1917. There was also the Decree on Workers' Control (November 1917). This recognised the takeover of the factories by workers.

War communism, 1918–21

Why it was introduced

The most immediate reason for the introduction of the war communism policy was **to win the Civil War**. Trotsky aimed to keep the Red Army well supplied and to feed the industrial workers in Moscow and Petrograd. War communism supplied them through forced requisitioning of peasant grain.

War communism also helped the Bolsheviks **enforce** their **authority** over peasant communities. During the Civil War, their support couldn't be relied on. The seizing of grain from peasants had the added advantage of terrorising peasants and preventing them from opposing the Reds.

War communism was a **socialist economic policy** — it involved the takeover of Russia's resources by the state. For example, the June 1918 Decree of Nationalisation announced the state's intention to take over all major industry within 2 years.

Furthermore, the rapid **deterioration** in the economy in spring 1918 suggested that a tough policy such as war communism was needed. Industry was falling apart because workers couldn't run the factories. The Civil War was causing serious shortages of raw materials. Industrial output shrank in the Bolshevik-controlled area. Peasants couldn't supply food to the cities at this stage, as there were no goods for which food could be exchanged. Finally, there was serious inflation, with food riots in many cities.

How war communism worked

War communism meant total communism — with no profit from the land or from business. There was to be complete state control of industry and agriculture. The following are the main features of the policy:

- Under the Decree of Nationalisation, the state was to take over all major industry within 2 years. Factories of ten or more workers were taken over by the state.
- The *Vesenkha* (Supreme Soviet of the National Economy) was set up to organise industrial production. It presided over the nationalisation of, for example, the banks and railways.
- Foreign debts were cancelled.
- The transport system was made less chaotic.
- Longer working hours were enforced in the factories, along with harsh discipline, such as the death penalty for strikes.
- Peasants would be forced to provide food to the government to feed the workers and soldiers.

Results of war communism

After years of economic problems, Russia could not afford complete overhaul.

Inflation rose dramatically. In 1920, the rouble was worth only 1% of its 1913 value. Steel production dropped from 4.3 million tonnes to 0.18 million tonnes in the same period. Electricity production by 1921 was down to one-quarter of 1913 levels.

The situation in agriculture was even more alarming. *Cheka* detachments known as requisition squads were sent into the countryside to take peasant grain by force. However, instead of forcing peasants to produce more grain, these squads had the opposite effect. Peasants, fearful of being attacked for having extra grain, simply produced even less. Between 1918 and 1921 an estimated 5 million people died of **starvation**.

All these problems led to the emergence within the Bolshevik Party of the **Workers' Opposition movement** (led by Alexandra Kollontai), which challenged the harsher aspects of war communism.

There was **opposition** to war communism from outside the party as well. The Kronstadt Mutiny of 1921 was a revolt in Petrograd by sailors who had supported the October Revolution but were now calling for more economic freedom. It was savagely put down. In Tambov, there was a peasants' revolt in 1920 and 1921. It was put down when the area was flooded with Red Army units.

In view of the fierce resistance inside and outside the party, Lenin decided to relax his economic policy.

However, the effects of war communism were not totally negative. The policy did help the Bolsheviks to **win the Civil War**. It also helped to support the Bolshevik advance towards a socialist economy, which Lenin saw as necessary if the revolution was to be complete.

The New Economic Policy (NEP), 1921 onwards
Why it was introduced
Opposition to war communism was emerging both outside the party and within it. While Lenin could not be seen to tolerate such opposition, he did recognise the need for economic change.

Problems in agriculture provided another reason for the NEP. Terror during the Civil War had forced peasants into producing less. As has already been detailed, **famine** gripped the country. Lenin therefore decided that if the peasants could not be forced, they would have to be persuaded to produce more.

A new economic approach was made even more necessary as food shortages contributed to soaring **inflation**. As we have seen, war communism had made inflation even worse.

Finally, a different economic policy was made necessary by the fact that industrial production was falling drastically up to 1921. In that year, coal production had dropped to less than one-third of what it had been before the First World War.

However, while Lenin relaxed some of the tight economic control that he had applied during the war communism years, he insisted that the NEP did not signify any weakening of his ultimate commitment to creating a genuinely socialist state.

How it worked
- Central economic control was relaxed.
- Peasants could make some profit from their produce.
- The requisitioning of grain was to be abandoned and replaced by a tax in kind.
- In the towns, small-scale business activities could take place. For example, private markets were set up, selling shoes and clothes.
- Large-scale business remained state property.
- Piecework and incentives were introduced, which allowed workers to buy food and improve their standard of living.
- A new rouble was introduced to combat inflation.

Lenin tried to justify the NEP by pointing out that for all the value of war communism as a socialist policy, it had failed to bring the increases in production needed.

Divisions within the Bolshevik Party
While the introduction of the NEP removed one major source of opposition to Lenin within the Bolshevik Party, it created another one. The Left of the party believed it

allowed the reappearance of a capitalist economy. Trotsky's views have been seen earlier.

Lenin, however, defended the NEP vigorously. He argued that he was taking 'two steps forward and one step back'. In other words, while Russia was progressing towards the ultimate goal of a socialist economy, a limited amount of capitalism was needed for a while. Lenin also reminded his Bolshevik comrades that 'the commanding heights of the economy' (large-scale industry, banking and foreign trade) were still in government hands. Furthermore, he insisted that the NEP would only be temporary.

Lenin also took a number of political steps in 1921 and 1922 to show that the grip of the party was strengthening rather than weakening. For example, by 1921 he had established a party bureaucracy across Russia, and 5,000 Mensheviks were arrested. In 1922 Russia officially became a one-party state. The Central Committee of the Communist Party became the sole instrument of power in the country. In the same year, Lenin announced a ban on factionalism. Shortly afterwards, Alexandra Kollontai was exiled.

Lenin won significant support for the NEP. Most importantly, he won over Bukharin. Bukharin, an economic expert and the editor of *Pravda*, became a valuable ally in the struggle to persuade the party to accept the policy. He urged peasants to 'enrich yourselves under the NEP'.

Results of the NEP
In **industry**, the NEP was a relative success. Coal production in 1921 was running at 8.9 million tonnes. By 1925 it had risen to 18.1 million tonnes. Steel production in 1921 was running at 0.18 million tonnes. By 1925 it had risen to 2.1 million. Meanwhile, electricity production increased from 520 million kilowatts in 1921 to 2,925 million kilowatts in 1925. By then, electricity production was exceeding pre-First World War levels. However, coal and steel production during the NEP still lagged behind the production rates achieved before the First World War.

Workers benefited from the greater availability of **food**. Ninety per cent of them continued to work in state-controlled industries. However, 'NEPmen' (successful private traders allowed under the NEP) controlled 75% of all trade by 1924.

The NEP brought relief to Russian agriculture. The grain harvest doubled from 37.6 million tonnes in 1921 to 72.5 million in 1925. However, progress was limited. Many peasants couldn't afford to buy the new machinery that was becoming available.

Peasants were in many ways better off. Quotas of food to be supplied by peasants were reduced. Since peasants were allowed to sell extra grain for a profit, wealthier peasants emerged, who were known as **kulaks**. Some of these became wealthy enough to buy more land and animals, and so increased the size of their farms.

Was opposition silenced?
Lenin's ability to be flexible in economic policy (by moving towards the NEP) had the effect of removing an important cause of opposition from outside the party to Bolshevik/Communist control.

However, it did not have the same effect on opposition within the party. In removing one source of opposition (the Workers' Opposition), he provoked another (Trotsky and other 'Left' Communists), which remained after his death.

Remaining problems after the NEP

Even after the NEP, there was considerable **difference between industrial and agricultural growth**. It took industry longer than agriculture to recover from the effects of the Civil War. In 1922 and 1923 an economic crisis (the **'Scissors Crisis'**) showed this.

There were also unbridged **divisions** within the party. The Bolsheviks were still divided over the merits of the NEP at the time of Lenin's death in 1924.

There were a number of big drawbacks to the NEP. It brought **no guarantees** of economic or political stability. There was still much to be done to modernise Soviet industry and agriculture. There was also great **uncertainty** within the party over how long the NEP would operate. Some party leaders doubted if it genuinely represented the aspirations of the Communist Party and the Soviet state.

Cultural life under the Bolsheviks

Focus questions

- What were the cultural values of Lenin's Russia?
- How did Lenin use propaganda and the arts to strengthen the Bolshevik regime?
- How important were propaganda and culture in helping the Bolsheviks to strengthen their grip on power?

What kind of culture were the Bolsheviks hoping to create?

For the Bolsheviks, a **Marxist culture** had to be one that honoured the Bolshevik revolution and the communist state. However, exactly how this was to be done remained unclear.

The cultural debate under Lenin

Constructivists and 'fellow travellers'

Those who favoured the creation through the arts of a new and better Russia became known as the **Constructivists**. They looked for new forms of cultural expression which showed the importance of the Soviet worker. The leader of the Constructivist movement was **Bogdanov**. One important Constructivist group was called Proletarian Culture (or **Proletkult**). This group enjoyed brief success between 1918 and 1922 in its efforts to create a new, working-class (rather than 'bourgeois') culture in the arts.

Lenin, whose tastes in the arts were quite conservative, had more pressing concerns on his mind than culture in the early 1920s. He took little interest in such radical new ideas.

Some other cultural figures were known as **'fellow travellers'**. These people were broadly in sympathy with the Bolshevik Revolution, but many were not actually communists themselves. Unlike the Constructivists, while they wished to promote the ideas of the October Revolution, they preferred older and more traditional forms of cultural expression. One such 'fellow traveller' was Mikhail Sholokhov, the author of the famous book on the Russian Civil War, *Quiet Flows the Don*.

Aspects of Bolshevik culture

Growth of state control over the arts (propaganda)
All of the arts were to reflect the achievements of Bolshevik Russia, and therefore of communism.

The Ministry of Culture
The Bolsheviks established the Ministry of Culture as a way of increasing government support for the arts. By 1924, the government had made an attempt to control most aspects of the arts.

Organised celebrations of the Revolution (propaganda)
The tradition of May Day parades was started in 1920. These glorified both the Soviet worker (1 May was a labour holiday) and the Soviet state. They took place every year. The anniversary of the Revolution was also celebrated every year. In 1920 a cast of 8,000 re-enacted the Revolution in a dramatic public spectacle.

Literature as propaganda
One famous Constructivist Soviet poet of the post-revolutionary period was Mayakovsky. He wrote slogans for political campaigns and posters, as well as pro-Bolshevik poetry.

There was also the work of the 'fellow travellers', whose position has already been explained above, in the sub-section on the cultural debate.

The theatre as propaganda
Two major works of theatre were produced during the post-revolutionary period. One of these was *Mystery Bouffe*, in 1918, written by Mayakovsky and produced by Meyerhold. The other was the re-enactment of the storming of the Winter Palace, staged in 1920 to mark its third anniversary.

The cinema as propaganda
Lenin believed the cinema to be the most important of all the arts for spreading Bolshevik ideas. One of the key figures in Russian cinema at this time was Sergei Eisenstein, although his greatest works were not released until after Lenin's death.

Music as propaganda
Shostakovich was one of the most famous Soviet composers of the 1920s and 1930s. However, much of the most distinguished work he produced was not published until after Lenin's death.

The use of *Pravda* for propaganda

Pravda was the official Communist Party newspaper. Founded in 1912, it became a vital organ of the Bolshevik state. Between 1917 and 1928 its editors-in-chief were Bukharin and Lenin's sister, Maria Ulyanova.

Throughout the Soviet period, access to *Pravda* was vital for party members. In the 1920s it moved away from its more intellectual stance of the 1910s and focused on issues concerning the Soviet worker. In the 1920s workers and peasants regularly wrote in to *Pravda* with reports on daily life.

Censorship

All the great figures in the arts had to walk a tightrope between expressing their own ideas and producing what they thought the government would want. The government had ways of enforcing its will. For example, in October 1917 the Bolsheviks closed down all the press and publishing houses that did not agree with their political point of view. In the middle of 1918 the whole opposition press was banned.

Another form of censorship was the State Publishing Organisation (or Gosizdat), set up during the Civil War. It was a method of exerting control over Soviet writers and other artists.

As a result of this tightening of control over the arts, two prominent artists, Chagall and Kandinsky, left Russia for western Europe.

Education

Constructivist experiments were tried, such as the Unified Labour School, which attempted a radical new form of learning through practical work and through labour. However, traditional (or 'bourgeois') educational methods remained the main form of instruction.

Elevation of women

Divorce was made much easier than it had been in tsarist days.

A women's section was created within the Communist Party, showing the new respect given to women in Soviet society. However, the leadership of the party continued to be strongly male.

Youth (propaganda)

Teenagers were channelled into the Communist Union of Youth of Russia. In 1920, there were over 400,000 members. It became a vehicle for socialist propaganda.

However, only after Lenin's death did this organisation become truly nationwide. By 1926, it was better known as the Komsomol.

Moves against organised religion

Up to 1917, the Russian Orthodox Church had been the official state religion. It had been financed mainly from heavy taxes on peasants and workers, and so was resented by many.

content guidance

Lenin considered religion a backward feature of the old tsarist government and believed it had to be removed. Atheism was one of the cornerstones of Bolshevik beliefs.

In 1918, the government decreed a separation of church and state. A number of measures were taken as a result. Church property and land was nationalised. The Decree on Land of October 1917 confiscated church land and distributed it among the peasants. The church was to play no part in education.

Furthermore, the government allowed churches and monasteries to be ransacked. At least 28 bishops and about 1,000 priests were murdered during the Civil War. However, in Lenin's time, no official anti-religious policy was adopted. The release of Patriarch Tikhon, the leader of the Orthodox Church, from imprisonment in 1923 reflected this.

Islam was another major religion in Russia, especially in central and southern areas of the country. It was the second biggest religious group after the Orthodox Church.

The government was relatively restrained in its activities against Islam. It was only after 1925 that the state began to take official action with regard to this faith.

Political changes after the Civil War

A number of political measures were taken after the Civil War with the aim of strengthening the Bolsheviks' hold on power.

The Mensheviks and Socialist Revolutionaries were outlawed in 1921. This proved that the Bolsheviks were now in a position to move against their opponents.

In 1922 the Central Committee of the Communist Party was established, along with a ban on factionalism within the party.

The other key event in 1922 was the creation of the Union of Soviet Socialist Republics (USSR). Russia absorbed the newly independent non-Russian countries into the USSR. These included the Ukraine and Georgia. Altogether, five countries were brought into the USSR.

The death of Lenin

In January 1924 Lenin died. He had been ill since 1922, and from this point his influence on government policy was limited. There followed a bitter struggle for his position as leader.

How Lenin helped the Bolsheviks

Lenin had achieved much, both in getting the Bolsheviks to power and as leader of the new Bolshevik state. He achieved what Lynch describes as a 'telescoped revolution'. In other words, he managed to achieve a **workers' 'revolution'** without waiting for the working class to grow in Russia.

Lenin successfully directed the first stages of a 'revolution from above'. He did this by establishing a **socialist dictatorship** at an early stage, which claimed to be acting in the interests of the workers of Russia.

While in power, Lenin pushed through controversial yet necessary measures which helped make the new Bolshevik state more secure.

He signed the **Treaty of Brest-Litovsk** against the wishes of the Left of the party. He also supported Trotsky's use of ex-tsarist officers in the Red Army. Stalin, among others, opposed this. Trotsky would not have got his Red Army measures through without Lenin's support — and the Bolsheviks might well have lost the Civil War.

Lenin's introduction of the **NEP** was also controversial. He persuaded a reluctant party to accept the NEP. There is a good chance that the Bolsheviks would have been overthrown if they had continued with war communism.

Finally, Lenin held out **against the idea of a socialist coalition** (coalition government with other socialist parties). Again, he had to resist opposition from leading Bolsheviks. This enabled him to shape the new state in the way he intended.

Stalin and the USSR 1924–41

The leadership struggle 1924–29

Focus questions

- To what extent was Stalin's victory in the leadership struggle due to his control of the Communist Party?
- How far would you agree that Stalin's victory in the leadership struggle was due to the mistakes of his rivals? (Tactical mistakes, policy mistakes.)
- To what extent was Stalin fortunate to become leader of the USSR by 1929?

The key figures

The main rivals in the leadership struggle were Trotsky (Red Army commander and Commissar for War), Kamenev, Zinoviev (Commissar for Foreign Affairs), Bukharin (editor of *Pravda*) and Stalin (Commissar for Nationalities). Trotsky was thought to be the favourite to succeed Lenin.

Stalin's problems

On the face of it, Stalin was confronted by a number of serious problems during the leadership struggle.

His rivals were much more high-profile and more established than he was. For example, Trotsky was Commissar for War and Bukharin was editor of *Pravda*. Stalin's main achievement of note was his part in the creation of the USSR as Commissar for Nationalities.

Stalin had played a very **limited role** in the October Revolution and had a poor record of service during the Civil War. He completely mishandled the situation in Georgia, suffering the humiliation of being removed from his military post. In contrast, Trotsky was a Civil War hero as commander of the Red Army.

One significant problem Stalin had was that he was **Georgian**. Russian was therefore not his first language, which limited him as a speech-maker. This contrasted sharply with Trotsky's outstanding speech-making ability.

Another difficulty facing Stalin in 1924 was his support for the **NEP**, which by the late 1920s was running into more and more difficulties. It was politically dangerous to be associated with it.

Worryingly for Stalin, Lenin expressed strong doubts about him. In his will in 1922, Lenin reserved some of his most severe **criticism** for Stalin, although most of the party's senior figures were criticised.

Finally, Stalin was **not a charismatic figure**. Between 1917 and 1924, he gained a reputation in the Communist Party for 'industrious mediocrity'.

Stalin's advantages

Stalin did, however, have some advantages as he entered the leadership struggle:

- He was one of the few revolutionaries with a genuinely humble background. Most of the others were from the wealthier classes.
- As Commissar for Nationalities, he was largely responsible for the formation of the USSR in 1922.
- His greatest advantage was his position within the Communist Party (see below).

Stalin outflanks his rivals, 1924–29

Stalin was able to outflank his rivals in three main areas, which can be loosely defined as personality, control of the party and sensible-sounding policies.

Personality

Trotsky

Trotsky was vain and complacent. This allowed him to make a vital tactical error — failing to justify his absence from Lenin's funeral. He was arrogant and made enemies easily within the party.

Partly because of this arrogance, Trotsky despised bureaucracy. However, Lenin had spent much time establishing a party bureaucracy in Russia. Stalin, on the other hand, was prepared to do the dull, bureaucratic jobs in order to gain power and influence.

It was not only the unattractive aspects of Trotsky's personality that weakened him during the leadership struggle. He had a high-minded approach to politics, a dislike of political scheming. This made him vulnerable to a more unscrupulous rival such as Stalin. Also, Trotsky was very loyal to the party. He therefore tended to accept decisions he disagreed with to avoid damaging it.

Stalin

Stalin liked to represent himself as unthreatening — a kind of 'uncle' figure. Within the party he gained a solid reputation. This drew support from those who feared Trotsky's power.

Stalin exploited his ordinariness. Described in 1917 by the Menshevik Sukhanov as 'a grey blur which flickered obscurely and left no trace', Stalin was able to use his ordinariness to disguise his ruthless ambition.

In reality, Stalin was totally unscrupulous. For example, he gave Trotsky the wrong date for Lenin's funeral. He exploited Trotsky's absence by playing a prominent role himself, delivering the funeral address.

Fortunately for Stalin, Trotsky failed to exploit the two major disadvantages that Stalin had:
- Lenin's distrust of Stalin, as expressed in Lenin's will (1922). The details did not come to light during the leadership struggle, largely because Stalin used his post as General Secretary of the Communist Party to prevent their release.
- Stalin's mishandling of the Georgian question during the Russian Civil War.

Stalin's control of the party

As **General Secretary**, Stalin managed to ensure that details of Lenin's criticism of him in his will were never released. He also used his position as General Secretary of the Communist Party to influence and control party members. He made sure they voted his way in the party Congress, in return for the promise of advance. Trotsky did not like such political infighting. This allowed Stalin to outflank him quite easily.

Furthermore, as General Secretary, Stalin was able to influence personnel in the party. He had a lot of control over the selection of delegates who were sent to the Congress. This helped him pack it with his supporters. Stalin also controlled party membership. He was able to get rid of party members who were more likely to support Trotsky, such as soldiers and students. In their place he introduced less intellectual people who were less likely to question him, such as young urban workers.

Crucially, Stalin won the support of Kamenev and Zinoviev against Trotsky. They were the chairmen of the Moscow and Leningrad Soviets (the two most powerful soviets in the country). The three men were soon operating as a collective leadership or triumvirate — one which excluded Trotsky. This helped Stalin to form a powerful anti-Trotsky bloc in the party from 1924–25 onwards.

As General Secretary, Stalin could present himself as the **true voice of the party**, and therefore he could blame any disputes on those who opposed him. Trotsky in particular was eager not to oppose party decisions. Nor were Bukharin and the 'Right' Communists willing to be seen to be causing disputes. All this played into Stalin's hands.

Policies
Foreign policy

Trotsky favoured the policy of 'world revolution'. He and other supporters of this policy claimed that the USSR would only be secure if the revolution spread beyond its borders. Stalin, however, put forward the concept of **'socialism in one country'**. This was based on the argument that the USSR must build socialism at home first, and could not afford to become caught up in damaging foreign wars.

Stalin won the argument. The party embraced 'socialism in one country' by 1925. His arguments made more sense for a number of reasons. Trotsky's 'world revolution' sounded too much like Menshevik policy. Also, throughout the 1920s there was an ever-present fear of invasion by the combined capitalist nations — a policy of 'world revolution' seemed to invite such an invasion.

Now Stalin turned on his former allies Kamenev and Zinoviev. In 1925, Stalin accused Kamenev and Zinoviev of supporting world revolution when they publicly backed the need for a workers' revolution in the capitalist nations. Now the 'Left' in the party was thoroughly discredited. In January 1925 Trotsky resigned as Commissar for War. In 1927 Trotsky, Kamenev and Zinoviev were expelled from the party. By 1929 Trotsky was exiled from the USSR.

Economic policy

The economic policy argument revolved around continued support for the **NEP**, as opposed to a policy of complete state ownership.

At first, Stalin supported the NEP alongside Bukharin, who had been the main spokesman for the NEP during Lenin's rule. Within the party, the 'Right' Communists wanted to continue with the NEP. The 'Left' Communists wanted to be rid of it.

By 1927 it was clear that the party on the whole had turned against the NEP. Therefore, in 1928 Stalin changed sides in favour of **complete state ownership**. This was known as the 'Great Turn' in his economic policy. He then turned on Bukharin and his supporters, leaving Bukharin isolated and discredited.

Why did Stalin embark on **the 'Great Turn'**? On a practical level, it made sense to move away from the NEP. During the agricultural slump of the late 1920s, hoarding of grain had reached worrying levels. Stalin realised this on a visit to the Urals in 1928. During this time, he encouraged poorer peasants to denounce kulaks for hoarding grain. This was the very beginning of his strategy to collectivise Soviet farming.

However, there was a more cynical reason for the 'Great Turn'. Stalin needed to isolate Bukharin, and his best chance of doing this was by exploiting Bukharin's enthusiastic support for the NEP.

There were a number of reasons why Stalin was successful in removing Bukharin and his supporters. First, with food shortages so severe in 1928 and 1929, it seemed to be no time to keep going with the NEP. The peasants' hoarding of grain meant it could not be distributed properly to those who needed it most. Second, the war scare atmosphere of 1928 seemed to make it essential to make the economy more productive (the NEP was not doing this). Third, Stalin was helped by the fact that Bukharin and his supporters were unwilling to divide the party.

In 1928 Stalin launched the system of collective farming and his first Five Year Plan (to modernise Soviet industry). This showed Stalin's commitment now to complete state ownership.

In 1929 Bukharin and his supporters Rykov and Tomsky were removed from the Politburo. They also lost all of the other key party positions they had held. By 1929 Stalin was undisputed master of the USSR.

Stalin and the economy

Focus questions

- How successful was Stalin's economic policy?
- How much transformation (change) was there in the Soviet economy under Stalin?
- What was the cost/gain for the Russian people from Stalin's economic policies? (Were the changes worth it for the people?)
- How consistent were Stalin's economic policies in 1924–41?

Economic aims after 1928

- Stalin aimed to create a totally socialist economy within the USSR. However, he was completely unconcerned about the human cost of this.
- Stalin's first priority once in power was to end the NEP. This had been partly a means of isolating his rival Bukharin in the leadership struggle. However, his 'Great Turn' from the NEP was also due to the problems it ran into during the agricultural slump of the late 1920s.
- Stalin was determined that the USSR should **industrialise rapidly**. The State Planning Committee (**Gosplan**) set targets to be met by every major industry in the USSR. This was part of Stalin's determined drive to establish a command economy in Russia. Rapid industrialisation was aimed at proving the superiority of the Soviet economic system over that of the west. It was also intended to help prepare for possible invasion by the west.

- In order to industrialise more rapidly, Stalin introduced his first **Five Year Plan** in 1928. By 1932 the first Five Year Plan had been completed, and Russia had made considerable progress in catching up with the west in industrial production.
- It was also Stalin's intention to **improve agricultural production**. A productive agricultural system was considered necessary to serve the country's growing industrial centres. Stalin therefore decided to collectivise Soviet farms, with a view to making them more efficient. This process began in 1928.
- **Collectivisation** was intended to 'socialise' the peasantry. They would learn to work cooperatively and live communally in the new 'socialist agro-towns' built for them.
- Stalin was determined that industrialisation and collectivisation would help him achieve 'socialism in one country'. In other words, he was convinced that they would help create a socialist economy that would enable the USSR to survive in the twentieth-century world.
- **Modernisation** was also a big economic objective for Stalin. In industry there was continued electrification, and in agriculture collectivisation brought more efficient farms and the introduction of modern machinery through machine and tractor stations (MTSs).
- Finally, Stalin aimed to **centralise the economy fully**, placing it all under state ownership. While big industries were already completely under state control during the NEP, agriculture was not. The establishment of large state-controlled collective farms from 1928 onwards was a way of doing this.

Economic problems, 1924–28

- In the late 1920s, the USSR was still suffering from the effects of the Civil War, as seen earlier.
- A more long-term problem was the limited nature of Soviet industry, as shown during the 'Scissors Crisis'. Productivity in key industries such as coal and steel in the mid-1920s was still behind what it had been before the First World War.
- Another problem was that the USSR was still politically isolated from most of the western countries whose technology they needed to access. However, Stalin partly managed to overcome this by attracting foreign economic and engineering experts such as Henry Ford into the USSR to help the country's industrialisation drive in the 1930s.
- The fact that the Russian economy compared poorly with the economies of other countries was another difficulty. France, for example, was still producing more coal and steel than Russia at this stage.
- Despite some early progress under the NEP, Soviet agriculture was still backward. An agricultural slump between 1924 and 1928 made the situation worse, leading to hoarding of grain by peasants and food shortages. Despite the new agricultural machinery available under the NEP, in 1927 there were still 5 million wooden ploughs.

- Another difficulty Stalin had to overcome was the fact that there were still some important supporters of the NEP in the late 1920s. Most prominent among these were the leaders of the Right of the party, such as Bukharin.
- There was also the problem of potential resistance to Stalin's policies outside the party. The kulaks, who had done well under the NEP, were a particular concern.

Collectivisation in agriculture

What is collectivisation?

Collectivisation means the fusing together of a number of small, privately owned peasant farms into larger, state-owned 'collective' farms. The people on these farms then work together in the production of food, sharing the machinery and surrendering the surplus to the state.

Why introduce collectivisation?

Stalin's views had been shaped by his visit to the Urals in 1928. This confirmed for him that the hoarding of grain, which happened during the NEP, had to be stopped.

Stalin wished to enforce state ownership in agriculture. This was the socialist solution for agriculture — effectively, agriculture was being nationalised. Collectivisation would 'socialise' the peasantry.

Stalin was determined to create **more efficient production** in agriculture. Collectivisation meant large areas of land could be farmed more efficiently through mechanisation. With this in mind, Stalin introduced Machine Tractor Stations (MTSs) to the countryside. He also intended to use experts to help peasants to farm more efficiently, using metal ploughs and fertilisers.

On a more personal level, Stalin was resolved to **destroy** the group of wealthier peasants whom he called **the kulak class**. He blamed the kulaks for having monopolised the best land, hoarded farm produce and kept prices artificially high — as well as stirring up resistance when the government tried to procure grain.

It was also essential to create a healthy agricultural system which would serve the USSR's growing industrial towns and cities. The new collective farms would get the grain to the cities and for **export** more quickly.

Finally, mechanised labour would also mean the number of agricultural workers could be reduced. These would then be freed up to work in the new industries in the cities.

The process of collectivisation

Tragically, Stalin's collectivisation plan did not just include the fusing together of small peasant farms into large state-owned 'collective' farms (**kolkhoz**) and the introduction of MTSs.

Indeed, while the NEP had revived flagging Soviet agriculture, from 1928 there was alarm about peasant hoarding of food, especially by the kulaks. Stalin decided to eliminate them. Their land was seized and they were deported, killed or imprisoned. They were the first victims of collectivisation and were targeted from 1928 onwards.

At first, violence against kulaks by neighbours was encouraged. Then the secret police were sent in against them (see below). Eventually (in the early 1930s), similar tactics were used against all peasants who resisted collectivisation. Anti-kulak squads (organised by the OGPU, successor to the *Cheka*) arrested and deported kulaks.

Reaction to collectivisation and early results

Many peasants burned their crops and slaughtered their livestock rather than accept collectivisation. As a result, almost half of all the livestock was killed in the USSR. This led to serious food shortages. In 1932 and 1933 there was famine. Ten million died. Historian Isaac Deutscher called the famine 'the first purely man-made famine in history'.

Two areas that were hit hard by collectivisation were the Ukraine and Kazakhstan. The Ukraine was one of the worst-hit areas during the famine, which was a bad blow as it was one of the richest areas of land in the USSR. In Kazakhstan 87% of sheep, 83% of cattle and 89% of horses were destroyed.

Eventual results of collectivisation

Collectivisation was consistently driven through by Stalin, despite some serious reservations from members of the party. In the late 1930s, he eased the pace of collectivisation, but by 1940 he claimed to have collectivised 97% of all peasant farms into collective farms.

However, the grain surplus that Stalin expected never happened. Although the famine had eased by 1939, agriculture continued to produce less than enough to feed the Soviet population.

Nevertheless, collectivisation did achieve its main aim — to provide the resources for industrialisation. The larger, mechanised farms gave agriculture the potential to improve (see 'Why introduce collectivisation?' on page 54). This was a genuine attempt to modernise farming.

Industrialisation through the Five Year Plans

Why were the Five Year Plans introduced?

As a Marxist, Stalin wished to move towards a **socialist economy**. The Five Year Plans were intended to create the large industrial workforce necessary for such an economy. There were bitter memories of the Civil War, which helped to spark off intense rivalry with the west, and Stalin's aim was to demonstrate the 'superiority' of socialism over capitalism.

Stalin was also determined to reinforce his credentials as **leader**. A successful industrialisation drive would help to establish him as Lenin's logical successor.

Industrialisation through the Five Year Plans was part of Stalin's attempt to **centralise** the Soviet economy. Gosplan, the state planning agency, took control of both industry and agriculture.

Introducing the Five Year Plans was also in line with Stalin's **modernisation** policy. For example, electrification was to increase and transport was to improve, particularly in urban areas.

Stalin realised that he needed to increase the USSR's **military strength**. He intended to make the USSR capable of resisting the threat of invasion from the west, particularly by Nazi Germany.

It was also Stalin's ambition to achieve **self-sufficiency**. With a strong industrial base, the USSR could produce the goods its people needed. Nevertheless, early on, the Five Year Plans needed foreign support, as in the case of the Dniepr dam.

Stalin had some aspirations to improve living standards in the USSR. Industrialisation generated wealth and could show the communist way of life in a good light to people in other parts of the world. However, while the second Five Year Plan was directed at increasing production of consumer goods, these plans had to be abandoned in the face of impending war.

Finally, in agriculture it was vital to increase grain supplies. Industrialisation would make available more accessible modern machinery for agriculture, which would help speed up production.

The Five Year Plans in action
The first Five Year Plan covered the period between 1927 and 1932. It concentrated on heavy industry. There was also an attempt to develop engineering, and a focus on developing machinery for both industry and agriculture.

The second Five Year Plan ran from 1932 to 1937. It also concentrated on heavy industry. There were attempts to develop transport, such as the building of the Moscow Metro. The chemical industry was also intended to grow.

The third Five Year Plan began in 1938, but was interrupted by the German invasion in 1941. Heavy industry continued to be important, and as war became more likely, the need for armaments became increasingly urgent.

Features of the plans
All three plans were characterised by:
- heavy industrial growth
- the fact that they were always declared complete a year ahead of schedule, to show the superiority of Soviet planning over capitalism
- the building of huge new industrial centres, mostly east of the Ural mountains, and so less vulnerable to attack from the West, such as Magnitogorsk
- spectacular projects to demonstrate Soviet might, such as the Moscow–Volga Canal and the Dniepr dam
- foreign participation, a feature of the first two plans in particular (despite their patriotic nature) — for example, Henry Ford helped the Russians to build a car industry

While heavy industrial growth and machine tool-making were consistent features of the plans, there was a slight change in focus in the second Five Year Plan towards transport, consumer goods (unsuccessfully) and the development of the chemical industry. During the third Five Year Plan, the focus shifted towards armaments production.

The process

Gosplan set industry particular targets (quotas) to be met over 5 years. The intention was to double or treble initial production in this time. However, no clear central direction was given regarding exactly how the targets were to be achieved. Another drawback to these Five Year Plans was that they concentrated on heavy industry.

Stalin used a variety of methods to motivate workers to succeed. Often he would use intimidation, but he would also promise rewards for successful workers. The most famous example of this was the Stakhanovite movement.

The Stakhanovite movement

This was a movement set up in 1935 to inspire or shame workers and managers to produce more. It was named after hero worker Alexei Stakhanov, a coal miner in the Don Basin, who on one day in August 1935 reportedly produced almost 16 times the norm of coal for a shift.

Successful workers could gain the title 'Stakhanovite', and as such gain better food, accommodation and other privileges, such as holidays.

An intensive propaganda campaign advertised Stakhanov's achievements, and workers initially responded very positively.

Cost of the Five Year Plans

Much of the implementation of Five Year Plans was carried out by the forced labour of Stalin's political enemies.

There was also extensive intimidation. 'Shock brigades' were used in factories to make workers reach quotas. Pressure was put on factory managers to fulfil their targets — failure to do so could lead to savage attacks from party officials.

There was also a cost in terms of the quality of production, as goods were rushed through in an attempt to meet or exceed targets. Faults often went unchecked. There was a significant loss of expertise, as key experts such as engineers and managers were deported.

Results of the Five Year Plans — how successful were they?

Effects on industry

Early on, workers struggled to meet the targets required, as they were so malnourished.

Eventually, however, industrial production rose dramatically. During the first two Five Year Plans, coal output went up from 35 million tonnes in 1927 to 128 million tonnes in 1937. In 1937, steel output was 18 million tonnes (second only to the USA), compared with just 3 million in 1927. For the same years the figures for electricity output were 80 million kilowatts compared with 18 million. Machine tool making and metallurgy also did well.

There were also outstanding specific achievements, such as the building of the Dniepr dam.

However, other sectors did not do so well during the Five Year Plans. Consumer goods still lagged behind the west. Nor did oil production reach the levels hoped for.

Furthermore, figures for production rates during the Five Year Plans may not be totally reliable. Local officials and managers tended to launder their production figures to give the impression of greater success. It was in the interests of the Soviet regime to embellish figures, to highlight the triumphs of socialism.

Quality standards also suffered, as stated earlier. Finally, the deportation of key experts deprived industry of valuable expertise (see 'Cost of the Five Year Plans' on page 57).

Effects on the Soviet people

There was little transformation in the quality of ordinary workers' lives. Rationing was in place until 1936. Living standards were dreadful in the industrial cities, and there were serious shortages of consumer goods.

However, perhaps surprisingly, there was widespread support for the plans among the Soviet people. Russians were, on the whole, proud to be a part of the Five Year Plans' many achievements. Many believed they were building a new and better society.

There was a significant demographic transformation. There was a spectacular relocation of the population from the countryside into the towns and cities.

Nevertheless, the Five Year Plans often relied on forced labour to make possible the big industrial and transport projects that were undertaken. Many of these, such as the Ladoga Canal project, cost thousands of lives.

Propaganda value to Stalin

Achievements were made to reflect the triumph of socialism. Magnitogorsk was a prime example — a city built from nothing by volunteers, including Komsomol members, peasants and herdsmen. Nearly half a million came between 1928 and 1932.

Literature, the arts and architecture were to glorify the achievements of the Soviet economy. Eisenstein advertised the successes of the Five Year Plans in his films.

There were significant improvements in urban transport, which were also used for propaganda purposes. The walls of the Moscow Metro (construction of which started in 1931) illustrated the triumphs of the Revolution and the USSR.

Stalin's political actions

Stalin's aims

Stalin was determined to make himself impregnable. He therefore took a number of steps:

- He moved to smash all possible rivals — something he achieved during his purges.

- He attempted to project an image of himself as infallible, using extensive propaganda and a personality cult.
- He reinforced his position in law, through the 1936 Constitution.
- He intended to make the Communist Party a reflection of himself. In the 1930s, communism in the USSR came to be known as 'Stalinism'.
- He was prepared to learn from earlier leaders of Russia how to keep power. He used and developed many of the methods Lenin had employed — for example extensive use of terror and the secret police — but he was also prepared to try a *variety* of methods to hold on to power. Force was important and effective, but so was propaganda. In the words of Isaac Deutscher, 'Stalin offered the people a mixed diet of terror and illusion.'

Terror

Stalin once said, 'One death is a tragedy. A million deaths is a statistic.' In this one statement, we can appreciate Stalin's contempt for human life and why he was prepared to destroy it with so little concern.

Why did Stalin introduce the purges?

Stalin was obsessive about removing all possible threats to his rule. The more powerful the person was, the more at risk they were.

The early purges, such as the purge of **economic leaders** between 1928 and 1931, provided scapegoats for the failure of the struggle against economic backwardness. Stalin was able to blame economic failures on economic leaders such as managers and engineers.

With the threat of war looming, these early purges were a useful way of arousing the patriotism of the workers against these economic leaders, who were accused of being 'wreckers' and traitors from within ('fifth columnists').

The purges were also a way of silencing the opposition that was developing within the party to Stalin's economic policies. In the early 1930s there was growing opposition to Stalin's treatment of the peasants during collectivisation. Others were worried that the Five Year Plan was falling short of its targets. The purges were a way of rooting out opponents to his policies. Kirov, for example, was known to be unhappy with the speed of industrialisation. Some in the Politburo were equally uneasy.

In the late 1920s and the early 1930s, Stalin was in the process of removing the **intellectual elements** from the Communist Party and replacing them with urban workers who were more likely to support him. The purges were a way of removing these intellectual elements for good.

At this time, Stalin saw a need to strengthen his grip on the party. In the early 1930s there were signs that it was loosening. For example, in 1932 Mikhail Ryutin attacked Stalin for being 'an evil genius'. Ryutin and his followers were then purged and expelled from the party. Even more worrying for Stalin was the situation at the **Seventeenth Party Congress** in 1934, where support among the delegates for Kirov could have threatened his position. However, by the end of the Congress he had consolidated his hold on power, and many supporters of Kirov later died in the purges.

It is also worth considering the purges as a logical extension of Lenin's policies. Lenin, like Stalin, had made extensive use of terror to keep control of the country. However, in Lenin's time, terror was only used against opposition from outside the party.

How the purges took place

Focus questions

- How did Stalin's purges help him to control the USSR?
- How important was terror as a means of helping Stalin to keep control over the USSR between 1928 and 1941?

The purge of economic leaders, 1928–31
A number of leading economic figures, such as managers, technicians and engineers (even planners), were targeted. These figures were branded as 'wreckers' and deprived of their civil rights and ration cards.

The murder of Kirov in December 1934 and its impact
There were a number of reasons why it suited Stalin for Kirov to die. Kirov had replaced Zinoviev as chairman of the Leningrad Soviet and built up a considerable power base for himself there. He was a highly popular figure within the party and had made a strong impression at the Seventeenth Party Congress in 1934. Unlike Stalin, he was an outstanding speech-maker. Furthermore, Kirov had had some concerns about Stalin's rapid industrialisation drive. Kirov was also opposed to the extreme measures being used to discipline party members.

There is a strong probability that Kirov's murder was approved, if not planned, by Stalin himself.

The post-Kirov purges
Stalin exploited Kirov's death by signing a Decree against Terrorist Acts, blaming the assassination on supporters of Trotsky. This led to a fresh purge of the party.

A large-scale round-up of people accused of being part of a murder conspiracy took place straightaway. These were then imprisoned or executed. Tens of thousands of others were deported. In 1938, Yagoda (head of the secret police, now known as the NKVD) was implicated in Kirov's murder, just before he was shot.

The Great Purge, 1936–38
The most serious threats to Stalin came from the top level of Soviet political life, so that was where Stalin started. He used various false charges to eliminate his party rivals, top generals and even NKVD leaders.

The Great Purge involved a process of punishment that usually followed a particular pattern. To start with, there was arrest by the NKVD. For most, the punishment after this was deportation to forced labour camps. These were run by a state body called the **Gulag** and were located mainly in Siberia. Altogether, 17–18 million people had been sent to these camps by 1937.

In the case of leading party members and military and police leaders, Stalin carried out **'show trials'**. During these trials, party leaders were falsely charged with crimes, usually concerning disloyalty to the party. They were forced to confess, after which they were made to commit suicide or executed.

Trotsky, now in exile, was usually blamed as the man behind all the alleged conspiracies against Stalin. Conspiracies were also often associated with the Nazis. Sometimes they were linked with both.

The **three great waves of terror** during the Great Purge took place in 1936, 1937 and 1938.

1936
The purge of the Communist Party leadership began in 1936, with the first great show trial taking place in August. 'Left' communists such as Kamenev and Zinoviev were convicted and executed.

1937
In 1937 the armed forces began to be targeted. The second great show trial took place in January 1937 and destroyed the army leadership. After it, Tukhachevsky, commander-in-chief of the army, was executed, along with seven other top-ranking generals. Also, 75 of the 80-man Supreme Military Council were executed. Marshal Gamarnik committed suicide in July. Political commissars were appointed to watch over the army.

Karl Radek, a leading favourite of Lenin, was convicted during the second show trial. Another victim was the veteran Bolshevik Pyatakov.

1938
The third great show trial took place in March 1938. It was followed by the deaths of a number of prominent figures. They included so-called 'Right' communists such as Bukharin and Rykov. Yagoda, former head of the NKVD, was also tried and shot at this time.

By 1939 only two of the nine original members of the Politburo were alive: Stalin and Trotsky. In 1940, Trotsky was murdered in Mexico. Of the 139 members of the Central Committee elected at the Seventeenth Party Congress, 110 were murdered. Of the 1,966 delegates to the Seventeenth Party Congress, only 59 lived to see another congress.

A new, loyal party leadership
Stalin replaced the old Bolshevik leadership with men who were loyal and not well known. One of these was Zhdanov, who replaced Kirov as chairman of the

Leningrad Soviet. Another was Khrushchev, who became chairman of the Moscow Soviet. Meanwhile, Yezhov replaced Yagoda as head of the NKVD.

A purge of the people

Soon these purges spread down through the ranks of the party and into Soviet society as a whole. The new head of the NKVD, Yezhov, began a policy of mass repression known as the 'Yezhovshchina'.

Particular groups were also targeted, such as the legal and academic professions and foreign communists living in the USSR.

No one was safe. Denunciations of people suspected of disloyalty were encouraged. After denunciation came arrest and deportation or death. An estimated one in 18 of the population was arrested during Stalin's purges.

Results of the Terror

It has been said of the Terror: '[By 1940] the revolution had finally devoured almost all its parents and a good many of its children.'

Stalin's position became almost impregnable. The purges helped him to remove his rivals and potential rivals. He was also enabled, through the show trials, to destroy his rivals' reputation. Finally, he was able to replace his rivals and potential rivals with those he knew would not threaten him. Leonard Schapiro calls the purges 'Stalin's victory over the party'.

Use of personality cult

Focus questions

- What were the main features of Stalin's personality cult?
- How did Stalin's personality cult develop in the 1930s?

It was Stalin's intention to represent himself as infallible. He employed an extensive personality cult to achieve this. His personality cult penetrated all aspects of Soviet life:

- Stalin's image appeared everywhere. It was shown on banners, coins and medals, displayed in shop windows and even sewn into pieces of clothing. There were statues of Stalin right across the USSR, in schools and town and city squares. There were images of him on mountain tops and in the Moscow Metro.
- Twenty-four cities and two provinces were named after Stalin.
- In the arts world, poems and songs were written in Stalin's honour. The wording of the new Soviet national anthem was altered to honour Stalin. Socialist Realist art glorified Stalin's role as leader.
- At least 24 different titles were invented for Stalin. He was described, for example, as the 'Grand Strategist of the Revolution' and the 'Greatest Genius of all Times and Peoples'.

- As time went on, there was a change in the nature of Stalin's personality cult. In the late 1920s, a careful effort was made to portray Stalin in the media as Lenin's logical successor — 'the Lenin of today'. However, by the late 1930s, the focus was much more on Stalin alone and his outstanding qualities.
- The extent of praise expected for Stalin is reflected in the fact that when one of his speeches was produced on a series of gramophone records, one side of one of the records was reserved for applause.

The personality cult was clearly successful in representing Stalin as an all-powerful, infallible leader, and it penetrated far and wide across the USSR.

The 1936 Constitution

Main features

The 1936 Constitution had a number of important features:

- It claimed that socialism had mainly been achieved — the USSR was now a classless society.
- Universal suffrage was established. However, the only party anyone could vote for was the Communist Party.
- Individual rights were recognised, such as freedom of speech, freedom from arbitrary arrest, the right to welfare provision and the right to education.
- However, the party's dominant position was left unimpaired. Schapiro has called the constitution a 'worthless guarantee of individual rights'.
- Less importance was given to the Communist Party as a whole, and more to the leading figures within the party. This opened the way for Stalin to dominate.
- Centralisation was another important feature. Moscow (Stalin himself) was now responsible for a wide range of policies, including the budget, foreign policy and defence.
- The USSR was now a federal state. Five more neighbouring republics were absorbed into it at this stage.

Significance of the 1936 Constitution

The introduction of the 1936 Constitution enabled Stalin to consolidate his position in the law. The domination that it gave him was so clear that it was nicknamed 'Stalin's Constitution'.

Propaganda and culture under Stalin

Focus questions

- What were the main features of Stalinist culture?
- How did Stalin use propaganda to strengthen his control over the USSR?

Stalin aimed to create a more socialist-orientated culture within the USSR. However, this was less important to Stalin than strengthening his own personal control.

Propaganda

Propaganda was an important method of control for Stalin. He once said, 'Print is the sharpest and the strongest weapon of our party.'

By the late 1930s Stalin had committed five sections of the Communist Party to the enforcement of propaganda. Cultural ideas were also enforced by groups linked with the Communist Party, such as the Komsomol, the trade unions and a number of cultural and sports organisations. One of these was the RAPP — the Russian Association of Proletarian Writers.

Cultural revolution

In the late 1920s, a short-lived cultural revolution took place, led by the Komsomol and RAPP. This happened at local as well as national level. It involved, among other things, the driving out of priests from towns and villages across the USSR, as well as criticism of writers and artists who failed to follow the Communist Party line. It was committed to the creation of the new 'Soviet man'.

Greater personal control by Stalin

By the 1930s there was major intervention in cultural life by Stalin. He stepped in more and more to bring cultural and intellectual activity into line with Communist Party policy.

Personality cult

The personality cult was propaganda concerning Stalin's own person. Unlike Lenin, Stalin made extensive use of the personality cult to strengthen his power. In fact, he even started a Cult of Lenin too. (Lenin himself had been against leading party figures putting themselves above the party itself.) Stalin thus effectively turned Soviet culture into Stalinist culture.

Cinema

Sergei Eisenstein emerged as a great film-maker. His films suited Stalin, as they glorified the achievements of the USSR in the 1930s (especially of the Five Year Plans), but they also glorified men on whom Stalin modelled himself, such as Tsar Peter the Great.

TASS

TASS was the official Soviet news agency, set up in 1925. It supervised the news agencies in all the Soviet republics and was the state agency most responsible for the distribution of information. It ran one of the biggest networks of correspondents in the world.

Censorship

The arts

Stalin wanted the arts to reflect his own greatness and the achievements of socialism. He saw these two as the same thing.

Futurism

At first, Stalin seemed to support Futurism. On the death of Mayakovsky (a Futurist and avant-garde figure in the arts) in 1930, Stalin proclaimed that Mayakovsky was 'the great poet of the Revolution'.

However, Stalin did not like the abstract aspects of the Futurist and avant-garde movement, which he later denounced as 'formalist'. He showed this when he condemned Shostakovich's opera *Lady Macbeth of Minsk*. This condemnation forced Shostakovich to produce less controversial music.

Others in the avant-garde movement were even more severely persecuted: Meyerhold, for example, was arrested in 1939 and died in prison.

Socialist Realism

By the mid-1930s Stalin had moved more towards the concept of Socialist Realism in the arts. This meant the encouragement of uncomplicated and ideologically correct work which honoured the Revolution and the Soviet system. In 1934 a decree was passed which officially promoted Socialist Realism. All original, creative work was shunned.

Stalin channelled writers, composers and artists into official unions such as the Union of Soviet Writers and the Composers' Union.

Religion

Unlike Lenin, Stalin adopted an official anti-religious policy in the USSR. The League of the Militant Godless was established in 1925 and lasted until 1941.

Stalin unleashed a wave of persecution against the Orthodox Church from 1929 onwards. He banned all its social and educational activities. Priests were persecuted. Collectivisation was accompanied by mass closing of churches and deportation of priests. By the end of the 1930s, only seven bishops were active, compared with 160 in 1925.

Nevertheless, Stalin failed to stamp out Christianity altogether. The outbreak of war in 1941 brought a temporary reinstatement of the church as part of his attempts to unite the country against the German invaders.

Closing down of mosques was also state policy under Stalin. In 1941, there were only 1,300 still open, compared with 26,000 in 1913. However, despite this, Islam remained relatively strong in the southern and central republics of the USSR.

Anti-Semitism

Stalin introduced into the Soviet Union anti-Semitic persecution on a scale not seen since the days of the tsars. He had the Jewish section of the Communist Party removed. By the end of the 1930s most Jewish schools, theatres, publishers and other institutions that promoted Jewish culture had been shut down.

Philosophy

In December 1930 Stalin told Soviet philosophers that it was necessary to 'rake and dry up all the manure' that had been spread on the issue of philosophy. Philosophers had to follow strictly Marxist (in other words, Stalinist) lines of thought.

History

In 1931, historians were instructed to study history along purely Bolshevik lines (in other words, the way Stalin saw it). They were told to dismiss Trotsky's role in the Bolshevik Revolution and promote that of Stalin.

Personal intervention

Like Lenin, he had conservative tastes in the arts, but while Lenin did not always enforce his conservative tastes, Stalin was much more inclined to do so.

Music

The works of many nineteenth-century Russian composers were frowned on as 'bourgeois'. This was part of Stalin's early inclination towards the Futurist movement.

However, there were limits to Stalin's new thinking in the arts. For example, the work of Prokofiev survived. Stalin was suspicious of anything he could not understand. He denounced Shostakovich's opera *Lady Macbeth of Minsk* in *Pravda*, the Communist Party newspaper, as 'muddle instead of music'.

Questions
&
Answers

This section contains four specimen exam questions. Each question is broken up into two parts. Part (i) is worth 8 marks and Part (ii) is worth 22 marks. Two specimen answers are given for each part of each question: an A-grade and a C-grade response. All the specimen answers are the subject of detailed examiner comments, preceded by the icon ⧉. These should be studied carefully because they show how and why marks are awarded or lost.

When exam papers are marked, a level of response is considered for all answers and then a precise numerical mark is awarded. Answers are marked according to four levels:

	8-mark parts	22-mark parts
Level 1	0–2 marks	0–5 marks
Level 2	3–4 marks	6–11 marks
Level 3	5–6 marks	12–17 marks
Level 4	7–8 marks	18–22 marks

Question 1

Part (i) Explain why Stolypin introduced land reforms in 1906 and 1907. (8 marks)

■ ■ ■

A-grade answer

Stolypin, Russia's prime minister between 1906 and 1911, was an intelligent politician who realised that the tsar's survival depended on his ability to make wise changes that could strengthen the stability of his regime. The land reforms were just such changes.

Stolypin's intention was to 'de-revolutionise the peasantry'. Essentially, he saw that wealthier Russian peasants could become a group who could help the tsar survive rather than threaten him. Satisfying such a group with the opportunity to buy their own land could, Stolypin believed, make them into a conservative political force. He called the process the 'wager on the strong'. As a result, new land, much of it in Siberia, was made available for purchase by such rich peasants under a voluntary resettlement scheme.

Another reason why such a move might make wealthy peasants less radical was that it removed them from the peasant commune (or *mir*). These communes often acted as hotbeds for radical discontent on the land issue. They were often visited by revolutionary political figures who passed on their anti-government views to the peasants.

Stolypin also appreciated that such a process could have benefits for Russian agriculture, making it potentially more efficient. At the turn of the century peasants in the communes tended to operate under a strip farming system, which exposed peasants to a very high risk of crop failure. Removing some peasants from the communes and allowing them to farm their own land meant the risks were reduced.

Stolypin also passed other land reforms which removed some of the serious grievances that peasants had against their landlords and against the government. In 1906 the hated land captains were removed. These officials had used ruthless measures to keep law and order in the countryside. Also in that year the passport system was ended, allowing peasants to move freely within the countryside. In 1907 Stolypin removed redemption (or mortgage) payments which peasants had had to pay to the government for their land ever since peasant emancipation in 1861. Redemption payments had been a major cause of the 1905 Revolution, so here Stolypin was removing a possible future reason for peasants to challenge the tsar.

✍ **Overall: This answer shows a very good understanding of the issues and the requirements of the question. It identifies the need to give reasons and not simply to list the reforms. It has a clear focus right from the start, and provides excellent detail throughout.** (8/8 marks)

■ ■ ■

C-grade answer

Stolypin was a good prime minister. He was repressive, but he also introduced some land reforms. Stolypin was known for his repression. He set up a new court system that made it easier for him to arrest revolutionaries. Over 2,500 were hanged after being tried in special courts. (Stolypin's necktie was what the hangman's noose was called.)

One of Stolypin's reforms was to give peasants the chance to buy their own land through resettlement schemes. This helped get peasants away from the peasant communes, which had been a problem. They often got revolutionary ideas in the commune, which was a dangerous situation for the tsar's government.

The land reforms were also good for agriculture, which wasn't strong. The communes had a bad system of farming the land, so getting them away from the communes could change this.

Stolypin wanted to prop up the tsar. He knew that the tsar's situation was weak after the 1905 Revolution and his best chance of surviving was to win over new groups of people to supporting the government — such as wealthier peasants. Stolypin called it his 'wager on the strong'. He hoped that by bringing in his land reforms, he could 'de-revolutionise the peasantry'.

Other land reforms were made, such as the abolishing of land captains and the ending of redemption payments. These made peasants' lives a bit easier, so they had fewer grievances against the tsar.

> **Overall: A number of reforms are covered in this answer, and some valid reasons for these are given. There is some development, but the answer is not always explained in enough depth. It lacks focus on the question at the start, and there is some digression early on.** (5/8 marks)

■ ■ ■

Part (ii) To what extent were economic factors responsible for the outbreak of the 1905 Revolution? (22 marks)

■ ■ ■

A-grade answer

Economic factors were indeed significant in leading to the 1905 Revolution. There were serious economic difficulties which helped create the worker and peasant discontent which made so many take part in the Revolution. However, these were not the only significant causes, as there were also political grievances, as well as immediate trigger events such as the war with Japan and the way the demonstration known as 'Bloody Sunday' in January 1905 was dealt with.

Certainly Russia was facing serious economic problems in 1905. There were long-term problems which hadn't been effectively dealt with. Russia had a very weak industrial base, with very few industrial workers. The vast majority of the population at the turn of the century (80%) were peasants. There was also an extremely inefficient agricultural system, based on strip farming – which helped expose peasants to widespread crop failure.

In addition to this, peasants laboured under the burden of heavy taxes and redemption payments for their land. This rural discontent continued afterwards, as peasants feared their land would be seized if they couldn't pay their redemption payments during the recession. The 1905 Revolution was the first time that industrial discontent combined with agricultural discontent.

Industrial workers began to suffer at the turn of the century as well. When recession hit, unemployment rose. Those who kept their jobs suffered poor working conditions (an average 11-hour day and not being allowed trade unions) and living conditions (poor housing). It was industrial workers who formed a large proportion of the protesters during Bloody Sunday.

The economic recession that began at the start of the twentieth century and lasted until 1906 made existing economic problems even worse. This created major unemployment problems.

However, economic problems were not the only factors that contributed to the 1905 Revolution. There were serious political difficulties as well.

Political problems were clear to observers well before the 1905 Revolution. In 1902 novelist Leo Tolstoy wrote an 'Open Address to Nicholas II'. In this, he pointed out his concerns about censorship, the denial of basic freedoms, prisons filled to overflowing and an army roaming the streets ready to shoot on a whim.

Tolstoy's comments reflect the tsar's determination to hold on to his autocratic power by force. Nicholas II was determined not to make meaningful political changes, as he believed democracy would bring about the collapse of the Russian empire.

The government system was corrupt and inefficient. Promotion was often achieved on the basis of nepotism rather than ability. This meant that there were few who were inclined to — or even able to — make the changes needed to stave off revolution in 1905. Prime Minister Witte summed up the situation in 1905 best when he said, 'The world should be surprised that we have any government.'

Nevertheless, even with these serious problems in the economy and in the political system, it still took two major disasters to spark off the 1905 Revolution — the Russo–Japanese War and Bloody Sunday.

The war with Japan in 1904 and 1905 was a national humiliation for the Russian government. Japan was considered an 'inferior' nation, and yet was able to inflict massive defeats on the Russians at Port Arthur, Mukden and Tsushima. The Treaty of

Portsmouth in 1905 marked the end of Russian expansion in the Pacific and at home prompted a general strike in September, as well as the formation of soviets in Saint Petersburg and elsewhere. Economically, it forced the rate of inflation up to 20%, making food shortages and discontent at home much worse.

Bloody Sunday was the event when, in January 1905, a crowd of peaceful protesters demonstrating for greater political rights and economic reform was savagely cut down by Cossack soldiers in Saint Petersburg. They had made economic demands, such as increased wages to meet the inflation problem. They had also made political demands, such as universal suffrage and freedom of speech. Over 100 were killed and 300 were wounded. Father Gapon, the leader of the demonstrators, in his despair cried out as the Cossacks charged, 'There is no God. There is no tsar.' The ruthless and cruel way that this peaceful protest was handled brought national outrage and was the trigger to a wave of unrest that came to be known as the 1905 Revolution.

However, it is worth noting that both the war with Japan and Bloody Sunday, as well as being causes of the 1905 Revolution, highlighted serious economic problems that already existed, such as shortages and inflation. Once again, this shows the importance of economic factors in the outbreak of the 1905 Revolution.

In conclusion, while other factors did play a big part in the outbreak of the 1905 Revolution, I would argue that economic factors were particularly important. They were at the heart of much of the discontent that surrounded many of the events leading up to 1905 and which triggered the Revolution itself.

> **Overall: This is a balanced, well organised and detailed effort. It is coherently argued and shows good detail and good breadth of knowledge. It makes a good link between economic problems and actual discontent. This answer shows fine powers of analysis and the ability to see, even in other causes, that there are economic issues at play — a good indicator of a top-level candidate. More development of the tsar's shortcomings as ruler is possible. Appropriate use is made of specialist vocabulary.** (20/22 marks)

■ ■ ■

C-grade answer

The 1905 Revolution happened because of a number of things. There were economic problems, but other things also caused it.

In January 1905, there was a big demonstration in Saint Petersburg known as Bloody Sunday. It was led by the priest Father Gapon. The demonstration was loyal to the tsar. It marched to the Winter Palace, with demonstrators singing hymns and carrying placards of the tsar. However, it was cut down by Cossacks, with over 100 killed and 300 wounded. The event caused horror in Russia.

There was another event that was important as a cause of the 1905 Revolution — the Russo–Japanese War of 1904–5. In this war, the Russians expected an easy victory over the Japanese, whom they saw as 'inferior'. However, the Russians were badly beaten. They suffered defeats at Mukden, Port Arthur and Tsushima. Tsushima brought the defeat of the Russian navy, which had travelled half way around the world to fight.

There were serious economic problems in Russia at this time. Agriculture was in a poor state. The strip system made it more likely that crops would fail. Peasants had to pay a lot of tax and also heavy redemption payments for their land. When crops failed at the end of the 1890s there was famine. Discontent grew, with rebellions in the Kharkov and Poltava regions in 1902. Discontent got worse after this, and a number of peasants became involved in the 1905 Revolution itself, partly because of redemption payments.

Workers were in a bad position as well. They suffered from poor living and working conditions, which the government did very little to improve. Industrial workers had to work an average of 11 hours a day. Housing was in a bad state in the cities, and unemployment was rising at the start of the twentieth century.

The tsar was a poor ruler. He preferred to spend long periods with his family rather than read government reports. He never wanted the job of tsar in the first place. He could be cruel as well, and particularly hated Jews. He refused to change the political system he controlled, believing that he should have total control over the country. He was heavily influenced by the Russian Orthodox Church, which was very much against change as well. The tsar wasn't helped by the fact that his government was not very effective.

In conclusion, economic factors were important in causing the outbreak of the 1905 Revolution, but other factors were important as well, such as political problems due to the tsar's rule, and trigger events such as the war with Japan and Bloody Sunday.

🖉 **Overall: This answer makes a range of valid points. It is balanced, with attention to the proposition, as well as other factors. It includes some good detail on economic problems and the tsar's weaknesses as a ruler. However, more focus is needed. It offers a little narrative at the start, but it lacks explanation and detail in places — e.g. on the Russo–Japanese War.** (14/22 marks)

■ ■ ■

Question 2

Part (i) Explain the short-term causes of the downfall of Tsar Nicholas II in 1917.

(8 marks)

■■■

A-grade answer

Russia's decision to go to war in 1914 contributed greatly to the tsar's downfall. This decision put massive pressure on Russia's industrial machine, which was still weak and dependent on foreign loans. This foreign assistance would be lost during the war. It also put her underprepared army under enormous strain — at the outbreak of the war there was only one rifle between three soldiers. Finally, it resulted in the loss of the royal family's considerable popularity.

During the First World War, Russian industrial output dropped by 50%. The area of land under cultivation fell by 20% (as peasants were conscripted into the army). Inflation rose by 400%. As a result of all these economic problems, industrial unrest grew to the extent that by the start of 1917 the number of strikes had risen to 1,330. One of these was the one at the Putilov steel works in Petrograd. This demonstration, which demanded wage increases to meet the rising food prices, was one of the trigger events to the February Revolution which brought down the tsar.

Within weeks of the outbreak of the war, the Russian army suffered massive losses, with more than 250,000 casualties at the Battles of Tannenberg and the Masurian Lakes. The tsar's decision to take command of the army in 1915 brought no real improvement and was followed by a further million killed in Galicia and elsewhere in Poland. The tsar was discredited now as a leader and no longer had his ministers to blame for his own failings.

While the tsar took command of the army, the tsarina took command of the government at home. She was in a weak position to do this, because of her German origins, and was soon (along with Rasputin) suspected of being a German agent. When she appointed Boris Sturmer Prime Minister in 1916, these suspicions increased. The tsarina was also under the influence of the ex-monk Rasputin. Although he had little expertise, his opinion often held sway when she made decisions on appointments and other matters. Between 1915 and 1917 there were 36 different government ministers, making for inconsistency and confusion in policy. Rasputin's corruption and immoral behaviour also discredited the monarchy.

The tsarina held out stubbornly against the advice of the duma or the zemstvos on how to run the country during the war. She determinedly held on to her autocratic authority. The contempt of the royal family for the duma (in particular, the closing down of the fourth duma in early 1917 — against which 80,000 protested) was another cause of the February Revolution. Opposition grew in the duma to the way the war was being conducted, and it was actually a delegation of duma representatives who, along with a number of generals, persuaded the tsar to abdicate.

> 🖉 **Overall: This is a thorough answer, well developed and with consistently good focus on the question. It provides an excellent level of statistical detail. A clear link is made between the problems that the country experienced and how these actually brought down the tsar. The answer includes a good introduction, although for an 8-mark question an introduction is not required, because of time constraints.** (8/8 marks)

▮ ▮ ▮

C-grade answer

Russia was weak going into the First World War. Its industry was relatively new and weak, and needed foreign loans. Russia was Europe's largest debtor nation in 1914. Its army was badly organised and it didn't have strong political leaders.

In the war, output dropped by 50%. Land was not used and less food was grown. As a result, food prices rose dramatically. A weak transport system meant that much of the food that was grown rotted in the train stations. There were serious shortages and discontent. There were 1,330 strikes in early 1917.

The war was a disaster for the Russian army. The troops were badly prepared to start with, with some not even having boots. They were also badly led. They suffered heavy defeats at Tannenberg and the Masurian Lakes. The tsar then took command of the army in 1915. He was discredited now as a leader and no longer had his ministers to blame for his own failings.

Meanwhile, the tsarina took over the government at home. She was German, and she and Rasputin were soon suspected of being German agents and having an affair. The tsarina listened too much to Rasputin. He got his way when she made government decisions. The tsarina changed her mind frequently, and appointed and dismissed ministers regularly. This was known as 'ministerial leapfrogging'. It made it very hard for government policy to be consistent. As well as this, Rasputin was known to be a womaniser and a drunkard.

The tsarina refused to pay attention to the duma. She believed in autocracy, as the tsar did. She closed down the duma in early 1917 because she didn't trust it. A lot of problems grew out of this, and soon duma representatives had had enough and persuaded the tsar to abdicate.

> 🖉 **Overall: This answer makes some valid points. It provides good detail on the tsarina and Rasputin, but more detail is needed on Russia's military defeats and economic problems. Greater focus is also required on the downfall of the tsar — the problems Russia experienced need to be shown to be causes of his downfall. The answer includes a sound lead-in, although an introduction is not required, because of time constraints.** (5/8 marks)

▮ ▮ ▮

Part (ii) How far would you agree that the role of Lenin was the most important factor in the success of the Bolshevik Revolution in October 1917? (22 marks)

■ ■ ■

A-grade answer

Lenin was a crucial figure in the success of the Bolsheviks in October 1917. He was the man who provided the ideology behind the Revolution, as well as the drive to carry it out. However, there were other reasons for the success of the Bolshevik takeover, such as the contribution of Trotsky and the weaknesses and mistakes of the Provisional Government.

It was Lenin who produced the *April Theses*. This provided the Bolsheviks with a political programme and a clear focus — something which other political parties in Russia at the time lacked. In this document, Lenin demanded an immediate end to the war and the handing over of power to the soviets which had sprung up over Russia since the start of the year. He called for 'all power to the Soviets'.

Lenin gave the Bolsheviks determination and drive, as well as a sense of urgency. He took them from being a disorganised shambles at the start of 1917 to being ready to take power in October. He managed to get the Central Committee of the party to accept the need for an immediate revolution against some considerable opposition, particularly from Kamenev and Zinoviev.

Lenin also pressed for the takeover of the soviets. As 1917 went on, it was becoming clear that the soviets were effectively running the country. Unlike the Provisional Government (alongside which they technically governed), they were elected bodies — so they had more authority. Military Order Number One gave them control of the army, while by the summer and autumn of 1917 they also effectively controlled communication and food supply. Regular attendance, in contrast with the other parties which formed the soviets, enabled the Bolsheviks to take control of the Petrograd and Moscow Soviets by the end of September.

Another important decision by Lenin was not to cooperate with the Provisional Government. Once again, this policy was not supported by other members of the Central Committee, like Kamenev. Stalin had similar views to Kamenev. However, Lenin's policy of non-cooperation helped the Bolsheviks to succeed, as they couldn't be blamed for the Provisional Government's mistakes — the only party that could escape the blame in this way.

Lenin was also quick to exploit the mistakes made by the Provisional Government. He exploited Kerensky's move to relax censorship in the spring to publish articles in *Pravda* that were strongly hostile to the Provisional Government. He exploited the decision of the Provisional Government to end the war and postpone land reforms with the slogan 'Bread, Peace, Land' — a slogan he stole from the Socialist Revolutionaries.

It is, however, important to remember that the contribution of Lenin was not the only reason for the success of the Bolsheviks, and neither was he always the assured leader he made himself out to be.

It could be argued that his handling of the July Days affair was weak. He proved himself unable to prevent a section of the Bolshevik Party from taking part in this ill-fated uprising against his wishes. The failure of the July Days briefly forced Lenin into exile and got Trotsky and other Bolshevik leaders arrested.

The role of Trotsky in the Bolsheviks' success must not be forgotten. He was the organisational force behind it. Trotsky played a key role within the Petrograd Soviet, rising to be its chairman in September as well as one of the three leaders of its Military Revolutionary Committee (MRC). The MRC carried out the military planning for the October Revolution. Trotsky was also commander of the Red Guard. The Red Guard was the only legitimate military force in Petrograd in October 1917, and it was they who took control of the city and stormed the Winter Palace, headquarters of the Provisional Government.

Trotsky was the best orator the Bolsheviks had, helping them to increase their popularity, accusing the Provisional Government of exploiting 'the bony hand of hunger'. He was also more well-known than Lenin. In February 1917 the Bolsheviks had 25,000 members. By October, they had 350,000. Much of this was due to Trotsky's popularity. He also gave experience to the Bolsheviks, as in 1905 he had been chairman of the Saint Petersburg Soviet.

Trotsky was also useful to the Bolsheviks as a voice of caution. While accepting the need for revolution as soon as possible, importantly he persuaded Lenin to wait for the right moment to carry out the assault on the Provisional Government.

Nevertheless, it must be remembered that Trotsky was a newcomer to the Bolshevik Party in October 1917. He only joined the party in the summer of that year, by which time much of the hard work in setting out the Bolsheviks' ideas through the *April Theses* had already been done by Lenin.

The Provisional Government must also bear some responsibility for its own downfall. Although it was in a weak position as an unelected caretaker government with serious economic problems to resolve, it also made a number of serious mistakes.

In the spring, the disbanding of the *Okhrana* by Kerensky and the easing of censorship gave the Bolsheviks a freedom to operate which they had never previously enjoyed.

The decision to continue the war led to military disaster in Galicia during the June Offensive (also authorised by Kerensky, as Minister for War), and wholesale desertions by peasants who fled the front lines to claim the land denied to them by the Provisional Government, which wouldn't introduce elections or land reforms until the war was over. After this point, the Provisional Government could no longer rely on the army for its protection.

Fierce repression of the July Days uprising and peasant land seizures, meanwhile, harmed the reputation of Kerensky and other socialists in the Provisional Government. It was harder now for them to claim that they were the friends of the ordinary working man.

However, almost certainly the biggest mistake made by the Provisional Government was its handling of the Kornilov Affair in August 1917. In response to the decision of Kornilov, commander-in-chief of the army, to march on Petrograd, Kerensky (now prime minister) turned to the Bolsheviks. He called on all the loyal citizens of Petrograd, including the Bolsheviks, to help him stop Kornilov. He released the leaders from prison and armed them. This gave the Bolsheviks a vital second chance at power after the July Days failure and boosted their popularity. The weapons they gained were later used to storm the Winter Palace.

Therefore, there is no doubt that a variety of factors assisted the Bolsheviks in their successful takeover of power in October 1917. The Provisional Government's mistakes were important, but it needed the Bolsheviks to be ready and able to exploit these, and Lenin in particular did this. Therefore, Lenin did indeed play the most important role in the success of the Bolsheviks in October 1917.

> **Overall: This is a very well detailed answer, with good explanation and a careful focus on why the Bolsheviks were actually able to succeed. It provides a good balance between Lenin's role and the importance of other factors, such as the role of Trotsky and the weaknesses and failures of the Provisional Government. It also handles the contrasts between Trotsky and Lenin well. The answer shows good analysis, especially of the Kornilov Affair and how it helped the Bolsheviks, although a little more analysis is possible in conclusion. The essay is well organised, with appropriate use of specialist vocabulary.** (21/22 marks)

■ ■ ■

C-grade answer

Lenin was a key figure in the success of the Bolshevik Revolution in October 1917. He made many contributions to its victory. He provided much of the inspiration behind it, as well as bringing a degree of ruthlessness and determination to the Bolshevik movement. This was essential for making sure they saw through their seizure of power.

Lenin wrote the *April Theses* on his return from exile. Now the Bolsheviks had a political programme to go by. Other political parties in Russia didn't have this. In his *April Theses*, he called for an end to the war and the handing over of power to the soviets. These were an alternative form of government to the Provisional Government. They had emerged throughout 1917.

Lenin was also very determined to hold the revolution soon and to make it succeed. The Bolsheviks were poorly organised at the start of 1917, but Lenin transformed them into being ready for power in October. Other leading Bolsheviks such as Kamenev and Zinoviev were less sure about the need for an immediate revolution, but Lenin managed to hold out against their view. Without this determination, the revolution might well not have succeeded.

It was very important to Lenin to take over control of the soviets. It was clear by the summer and autumn of 1917 that they were practically running the country. By the autumn these bodies controlled many of the essential elements of government, such as food supplies and communications. Military Order Number One, issued in March, gave them authority over the army as well. The Bolsheviks attended the soviets regularly, which allowed them to control the two main soviets of Russia — the Moscow and Petrograd Soviets — by the end of September.

Non-cooperation with the Provisional Government was another policy of Lenin's which helped the Bolsheviks to take power. As a result of this, the Bolsheviks couldn't be blamed for the Provisional Government's mistakes. As all the other major socialist and liberal parties were represented in the Provisional Government, they couldn't avoid the blame for its failings. Once again, Lenin had to overcome significant opposition to this strategy — from Kamenev and Stalin in particular — but he had the resolve to force it through.

Therefore, Lenin made a number of very important contributions to the success of the October Revolution, and was vital to its success.

> ✍ **Overall: This answer offers a very well detailed explanation of the role of Lenin. It is particularly well detailed on the importance of the takeover of the soviets. It has a focused introduction, and that focus is maintained through the rest of the essay. Crucially, though, this essay is not balanced. No attention is given to the roles of others, such as Trotsky, and very limited attention is given to the Provisional Government.** (14/22 marks)

> ✍ **NB Do not rely on both revolutions being covered in Question 2. It may well be that they form a part-question in Question 2 and a part-question in Question 3.**

■ ■ ■

Question 3

Part (i) Explain the Bolsheviks' main political objectives between 1917 and 1924.

(8 marks)

■ ■ ■

A-grade answer

The Bolsheviks aimed to establish a dictatorship in Russia, and did so as soon as they took power in 1917. It was to be, in their words, a 'Dictatorship of the Proletariat' — that is, one which would rule in the interests of the working man. Lenin believed that dictatorship was necessary in Russia, as the revolution was not yet complete and so the Russian people were not yet fit to rule themselves.

Another of Lenin's most immediate aims was for Russia to become a soviet socialist republic. He declared his intention to do this in his *April Theses* in 1917. Russia was declared a soviet socialist republic in the 1918 Constitution. Later, in 1922, the Union of Soviet Socialist Republics (USSR) was declared, which included Russia and five other republics.

However, it would not be until 1922 that Russia could be called a truly one-party state. This was another key objective of the Bolsheviks. For this to happen, the Bolsheviks needed to remove the threat from their opposition. The Bolsheviks faced fierce opposition from a variety of political groups — tsarists, democratic politicians (such as the Kadets and the Octobrists), as well as revolutionary parties such as the Socialist Revolutionaries. There was also resentment from Russia's abandoned First World War allies. All these groups came together as the Whites to fight the Bolsheviks (the Reds) in the Russian Civil War.

Ending the war with Germany was another political objective of the Bolsheviks. In reality, the Bolsheviks had little choice, with mass desertions from the army in summer 1917 and German troops on Russian soil after this. Therefore, the Treaty of Brest-Litovsk was signed in March 1918. This ended Russia's involvement in the First World War.

It was important to Lenin to extend the control of the Bolshevik Party across Russia. With this aim in mind, a party bureaucracy was set up across much of the country by 1921. Greater central control was established when the Central Committee of the Communist Party was set up in 1922.

In foreign policy, Lenin's ultimate aim was world revolution. The Bolsheviks hoped that victory in the Civil War would encourage Russia's neighbours to become communist as well. Trotsky believed that the Revolution would only be secured by having friendly (meaning communist) neighbours.

🖉 **This answer provides very good detail and explanation. A little more development of the 'world revolution' concept is possible. The answer has a good focus on objectives and is well developed in areas such as the opposition faced by the Bolsheviks. It is set well into the context of the time, with reference to key events.** (7/8 marks)

■ ■ ■

C-grade answer

The Bolsheviks intended to set up a 'Dictatorship of the Proletariat' as soon as they won power. This would be a government that would rule in the interests of the working people of Russia until a genuinely socialist state had been achieved. In 1917 the Russian people were not 'politicised' to accept Marxist ideas (or even literate in most cases), and so were not ready to rule themselves as Marx had predicted they ultimately would.

The Bolsheviks also aimed to remove the significant opposition that they faced in 1917. This opposition came from many directions. There were supporters of the tsar, who was still alive and still in Russia. There were democratic politicians. There were socialist parties that opposed the Bolsheviks, such as the Socialist Revolutionaries and the Mensheviks. Also, Russia's former First World War allies opposed the Bolsheviks. They were angry at the Bolsheviks for ending Russia's participation in the First World War. These groups joined together to become the Whites. The Whites fought the Bolsheviks (the Reds) in the Russian Civil War.

It was also an objective of the Bolsheviks to establish a soviet socialist republic.

🖉 **This answer has some good early development, especially on the extent of opposition to the Bolsheviks. It shows a clear grasp of why the Bolsheviks wanted to establish a dictatorship — a key political objective. There are, however, gaps in knowledge, for example on issues such as ending the war and establishing a party bureaucracy.** (5/8 marks)

■ ■ ■

Part (ii) 'The success of the Bolsheviks in the Russian Civil War between 1918 and 1921 was due to Trotsky more than any other factor.' To what extent do you agree with this verdict? (22 marks)

■ ■ ■

A-grade answer

The success of the Bolsheviks between 1918 and 1921 was due to a number of factors. Trotsky's role was more important than other factors, because he directed and organised the Red Army in an effective way which was not matched by the White generals.

Trotsky played a major role in the organisation of the Red Army. Through conscription, he brought the numbers of the Red Army up to 5 million. He integrated former tsarist officers into the Red Army (which was in a shambolic state up to that point) to train his men. A strong strain of discipline was introduced, with saluting, ranks and an end to the election of officers. Political commissars were introduced to army units, who would report back to headquarters and ensure that the officers acted in a politically correct way. Finally, the death penalty was introduced for a range of offences (particularly desertion or disloyalty). This didn't stop desertions from taking place, but it did make sure that those who stayed in the Red Army performed well.

Trotsky had clear objectives. His priorities were to keep his army supplied and to prevent the Whites from gathering together in one place in large numbers. Their political objective was equally clear: to defend the Bolshevik revolution. This contrasted to the Whites, who had conflicting political priorities.

Trotsky was an inspirational leader. He played a dynamic role in the Civil War. Far from being a backroom commander, he used his specially equipped train to rush to the parts of Russia where the fighting was fiercest to urge on his men. On his arrival, he supplied his men with their military needs, as well as encouraging them with his rousing speeches — in a way that the White commanders were not capable of.

Trotsky also made some important tactical decisions. One of these was his decision to defend Petrograd when it was in danger of falling to Yudenich. This was an important move for morale — refusing to abandon the 'home of the revolution'. Other leading Bolsheviks were prepared to surrender the city.

Trotsky's Red Army also played a key role, along with the *Cheka*, in the 'Red Terror', which terrorised peasant communities into not opposing the Bolsheviks.

However, it was not only Trotsky who contributed to the success of the Reds in the Russian Civil War. Lenin also played an important role. Furthermore, the Whites were weak and contributed greatly to their own defeat.

Lenin's contribution to the Red propaganda campaign was very important. He got an appealing message across, portraying the Reds as patriotic defenders of Russia against those who were in league with 'foreign interventionists'. He, alongside Alexandra Kollontai, made effective use of picture propaganda with a population where the majority could not read or write.

Lenin also supported the key decisions made by Trotsky, such as the decision to bring the former tsarist officers into the Red Army. He forced this through against much opposition from within the party.

Lenin's economic policy, war communism, also helped win the Civil War. This kept the Red Army and the city workers well supplied. These supplies were made possible by the forced requisition of grain from the peasants.

Lenin, alongside Trotsky, operated the 'Red Terror'. In this terror campaign, *Cheka* squads were used to terrorise (and sometimes even destroy) entire peasant communities. It stopped neutrals in the countryside opposing the Reds.

It should be pointed out, however, that Lenin's role was mainly a supportive role to that of Trotsky.

Attention also needs to be given to the weaknesses and mistakes of the Whites in the Civil War. The Whites were politically divided. They were a combination of tsarists, constitutional politicians, Socialist Revolutionaries and foreign troops. The foreign troops in the north (who supported democracy), for example, fell out with Kolchak, who was a tsarist. On the other hand, the Reds had a single, clear political goal: to defend the Revolution. The Whites were also geographically divided, and so easily picked off by the Reds, who controlled the key industrial and transport centres and so had central control of the country.

It also harmed the Whites that they were badly outnumbered. The White army never rose to more than a third of a million men. The Red Army reached 5 million, thanks to forced conscription.

The Whites depended on foreign countries for their supplies. These supplies were not enough and were also sometimes wasted. The Whites were now even more open to the accusation that they were on the side of foreigners, as opposed to the patriotic Reds. Their reputation was further damaged by being associated with Russia's pre-revolutionary past.

The Whites were very poorly disciplined and poorly organised. Marshal Denikin said of his men once, 'I can do nothing with my army. I am glad when it carries out my combat orders.' In Omsk, White army uniforms were sold on the black market and the troops lived in brothels in a haze of cocaine and vodka. This was in sharp contrast to the tight discipline of the Reds.

It was impossible for the Whites to exploit the cruelty of the Reds, as they behaved no better themselves. In the south, for example, Cossacks raped large numbers of women and murdered huge numbers of Jews.

Therefore, overall, Trotsky indeed played the most important role in helping the Bolsheviks win the Civil War, as he organised, disciplined and inspired the Reds in a way that the White generals never could do. Lenin's role was significant, but was only a supportive one.

> **Overall: This is a well-organised and coherently argued answer, with excellent knowledge of the period. It makes appropriate use of specialist vocabulary. It shows a good early focus on the question, and this clear focus is maintained throughout. It is well balanced, with detailed consideration of both the proposition and other factors. It brings out well the contrast between the strengths of the Reds and the corresponding weaknesses and mistakes of the Whites. It provides a well-summarised conclusion. The role of Lenin could be slightly more developed.** (21/22 marks)

C-grade answer

I would agree that Trotsky was mainly responsible for Bolshevik success in the Civil War to a very great extent. Trotsky organised the Reds, and he also commanded the Red Guard. However, Lenin played a supportive role. The weaknesses of the Whites also assisted the Bolsheviks.

Trotsky kept control of the Reds, and he kept them fighting for one clear reason — to defend the Bolshevik revolution. He kept his aims clear and simple — to stop the Whites advancing.

Trotsky gave the Reds a lot of discipline. He put political commissars into each army unit. He ended elections of officers and introduced ranks again. There was the death penalty for quite a few offences.

Trotsky commanded the Red Guards. They were the only legal force in Petrograd, and stormed the Winter Palace in Petrograd, helping the Bolsheviks secure more control. By this stage, other military forces had deserted Petrograd, and the Winter Palace was defended by only a small detachment of Cossacks and a women's battalion.

Trotsky had a huge personality, which helped to inspire the Reds in the Civil War. He was a dynamic figure, dashing to where the fighting was fiercest in his specially armoured train. When he arrived, he would inspire his men. He made an important decision to defend the capital Moscow. It was thought that Kolchak would succeed, but Trotsky won.

Trotsky ensured that the Bolsheviks had control of the two main industrial and administrative centres, as well as the transport network. This helped the Reds to supply their men, while the Whites couldn't do this.

However, Lenin also played an important supportive role to Trotsky. Trotsky was also helped by the weaknesses of the Whites.

Some of the Whites were in such remote places that they couldn't have much of an effect on the war. The Whites were spread far apart. They were easily picked off by Trotsky. They also had different political views, with some wanting democracy and others wanting a return of the tsar.

The Whites were not well organised. As a result, they couldn't make the most of the 'Red Terror'. They were a shambles. Soldiers sometimes lived in brothels and drank too much vodka. Some sold their uniforms on the black market. Many didn't care about the cause.

The Whites had not got as many men as the Reds. The Reds had 5 million men, due to forced conscription. The Whites never had more than a third of a million.

The Reds also made sure that many didn't oppose them — through the 'Red Terror'. They sent squads into the countryside to terrorise the peasants.

In conclusion, I think Trotsky was the main reason why the Bolsheviks succeeded in the Civil War. He disciplined his troops. He kept them well organised. There were other factors as well, but Trotsky was the most important.

> Overall: This answer has a strong focus on the proposition and is quite clearly argued. It manages to achieve a balance, with both the proposition and other factors investigated. It reveals some gaps in knowledge, particularly on Lenin, e.g. with regard to war communism. More detail could have been provided on the Whites. It suffers from vagueness in places and a little inaccuracy (e.g. Kolchak/Denikin). There is also some digression, and some confusion between the October Revolution and the Russian Civil War.   (15/22 marks)

■ ■ ■

Question 4

Part (i) Explain Stalin's economic objectives between 1928 and 1941. (8 marks)

■ ■ ■

A-grade answer

First, Stalin wished to end the NEP. The NEP had been running into difficulties in the late 1920s, and peasant hoarding of grain was common, as Stalin himself discovered on a visit to the Urals in 1928. Abandoning the NEP would also give Stalin the opportunity to isolate his rival Bukharin and the 'Right' Communists, who continued to support the policy.

During the leadership struggle, Stalin's foreign policy had been based on the concept of 'socialism in one country'. The building of a socialist economy within the USSR would require rapid industrialisation and a state-controlled agricultural system.

Industrialisation was also very important to Stalin. Rapid industrialisation would, he believed, prove the superiority of the socialist system over capitalism. It would also, in his mind, give the USSR the capacity to withstand invasion from the west, and particularly the Germans, as seemed increasingly likely during the 1930s. Therefore, a series of Five Year Plans were carried out to achieve rapid industrial growth, starting in 1928.

Stalin intended to collectivise agriculture — in other words, create large state-controlled collective farms. Agricultural improvement and growth would, Stalin hoped, feed the growing population of industrial workers in the cities. Industrial growth was, however, given priority. Stalin also hoped to 'socialise' the peasantry, by requiring them to live and work communally. For this purpose collective farms were established, as were 'agro-towns' for the peasants to live in. The kulaks — whom Stalin blamed for the hoarding of grain in the late 1920s — were deported. This process began in the late 1920s and continued into the early 1930s.

Modernisation was also one of Stalin's economic objectives. New machinery was brought to the countryside through machine and tractor stations, while electrical output soared during the first two Five Year Plans.

> 🖉 **This is a well-informed answer, providing a good focus on economic objectives rather than simply detailing economic policy. Economic objectives are put into the historical context well. The answer gives coherent explanations, although more development would occasionally be possible, for example regarding the anti-kulak squads. More explanation is possible of the 'socialism in one country' concept.** (7/8 marks)

■ ■ ■

C-grade answer

Stalin wished to make the economy of the USSR strong. He wanted to prove to the rest of the world that a socialist economy could be more successful than a capitalist one. He wanted to centralise the economy and bring it under the control of the government. It was important for it to produce as much as possible.

Stalin wished to improve agriculture. He intended to introduce large farms into the countryside which would produce more.

Soviet agriculture had been going through a bad time in the late 1920s. Much of the countryside was without the machinery it needed. In 1927, for example, there were still 5 million wooden ploughs.

To make the economy more productive, Stalin introduced his Five Year Plans. These aimed to boost production in particular areas within 5 years. There was a big focus on heavy industry at the start, and later on getting the USSR ready for war. Stalin believed it was inevitable that the USSR would be invaded by Germany.

> ✍ **This answer makes a number of valid points, but more development is needed. It is vague in places, for example on collectivisation. There is some lack of focus on economic objectives, but the subject of the Five Year Plans is quite well developed.** (5/8 marks)

■ ■ ■

Part (ii) 'Terror was the most important means by which Stalin consolidated his power in the USSR between 1928 and 1941.' To what extent do you agree with this statement? (22 marks)

■ ■ ■

A-grade answer

Terror was an important way for Stalin to strengthen his power in the USSR between 1928 and 1941. Stalin used other methods as well, such as propaganda, but almost certainly terror was the most important method.

While the Great Purge was the most devastating way of using terror in this period, terror was also used against the Soviet people in other ways. In the factories, 'shock brigades' were used to push workers to achieve their industrial targets. If managers (who were put under constant pressure by party officials) failed to reach their targets, they were branded as 'wreckers' and 'saboteurs', and ran the risk of being deported.

Meanwhile, in the countryside, anti-kulak squads (part of the secret police, the OGPU) were used in Stalin's attempts to destroy the kulak class.

Purges were, however, the main form of terror used by Stalin. Between 1928 and 1931 there was a purge of the economic leaders of the USSR. These economic leaders included engineers, factory managers and technicians. As a result, many of these people were stripped of their ration cards. Given the food shortages at the time, this was in some cases a sentence of death.

When Ryutin attacked Stalin in public as an 'evil genius' in 1932, he and his followers within the Communist Party were purged — they were expelled from the party.

It was the murder of Kirov — almost certainly on Stalin's orders — in December 1934, however, that led to the most savage spell of purges. Kirov was the Communist Party boss in Leningrad. He was a very popular figure within the party. He was an outstanding orator and outshone Stalin at the Seventeenth Party Congress of 1934 — a blow to Stalin's efforts to remain outright leader. All of this had made Kirov a big threat to Stalin.

Cleverly, Stalin managed to put the blame for Kirov's murder on his enemies. He passed a Decree against Terrorist Acts, which enabled him to begin a wave of purges against his rivals — particularly Trotsky's supporters. Thousands were deported.

Nevertheless, it was the Great Purge of 1936 to 1939 which did the most to make Stalin's position impregnable. In August 1936 the first great show trial took place. After this the leading 'Left' Communists, including Zinoviev and Kamenev, were shot.

In 1937 the focus turned on the armed forces. A second major show trial took place in January, with Tukhachevsky, the commander-in-chief of the army, being executed afterwards, as well as seven other leading generals. Marshal Gamarnik committed suicide. There were also two prominent non-military casualties – Radek (who had been a loyal supporter of Lenin) and the veteran Bolshevik Pyatakov.

After the third show trial of March 1938, it was the turn of the 'Right' Communists such as Bukharin to be shot, as well as the head of the NKVD, Yagoda.

The purges then extended to all levels of society, with one out of every 18 Soviet citizens being arrested.

Schapiro describes the purges as 'Stalin's victory over the party'. They removed rivals, destroyed their image (through the show trials) and led to the emergence of loyal followers of Stalin, such as Khrushchev and Zhdanov (who replaced Kirov as party boss in Leningrad).

However, terror was not the only method that Stalin used to control the USSR. Propaganda was also very important to him.

Stalin devoted five sections of the Communist Party to propaganda. He used organisations linked to the party, such as the RAPP and the Komsomol, to spread propaganda. These groups were particularly prominent, for example, during the short-lived cultural revolution of the late 1920s and early 1930s.

Stalin once said, 'Print is the sharpest and the strongest weapon of our party.' The arts and the media were therefore carefully controlled, often under Stalin's personal direction.

In the arts, after briefly paying lip-service to the ideas of the Futurist and avant-garde movements (for instance, describing Mayakovsky on his death in 1930 as 'the great poet of the Revolution'), Stalin imposed his own concept of 'Socialist Realism' on the arts. This involved shunning abstract art and focusing on art which was uncomplicated and glorified socialism. In 1934 a Decree on Socialist Realism was passed. Stalin was prepared to impose his Socialist Realist tastes personally, dismissing Shostakovich's opera *Lady Macbeth of Minsk* as 'muddle instead of music' in an article in *Pravda.*

The Union of Soviet Writers and the Composers' Union were established as a way of controlling leading writers and composers and forcing them to toe the government line in their work.

In the media, *Pravda* practically became a mouthpiece of Stalin's views. The Soviet news agency TASS distributed Stalin's views throughout all the republics of the USSR and ran one of the biggest networks of correspondents in the world.

Stalin made extensive use of personal propaganda, through his personality cult. This was successful in giving Stalin an image of infallibility and penetrated all aspects of Soviet life. Twenty-four cities and two provinces were named after Stalin. Statues of him were built in all the major cities and towns of the USSR. In the media, he was portrayed firstly as 'the Lenin of today', and then, as the 1930s wore on, as an outstanding figure in his own right with superhuman qualities. Poems and songs were composed in Stalin's honour. Even the words of the national anthem were changed to praise Stalin. He went under a number of flattering titles, such as the 'Grand Strategist of the Revolution' and the 'Greatest Genius of all Times and Peoples'. Meanwhile, on the farms, the tractors produced in the 1930s were called 'Stalinettes'.

Another area where Stalin imposed his control was the 1936 Constitution. Here he reinforced his position in the law. In what was known as 'Stalin's Constitution' because of the influence he had over it, Stalin was able to strengthen the role of the leading figures in the Communist Party (meaning himself) and the Communist Party itself. The Constitution also gave Stalin more central control over matters such as the budget. Stalin's domination was so great that he was even able to afford to give guarantees of a number of individual human rights (guarantees he didn't keep), such as freedom of speech.

In conclusion, I would say that while other factors were very important to Stalin, such as propaganda, it was his use of terror which was the most important reason why he was able to prevent opposition to him and be secure in power.

> ✍ **Overall: This is a very well-explained and developed answer. It is coherently expressed. It includes a very good range of detail, for example on the purges and Stalin's personality cult. It is balanced, with detailed attention both to the proposition and to other factors, such as propaganda as a method of control of the USSR. There is excellent detail and focus on the question throughout. Economic control could be explored — for example, the Stakhanovite movement.** (21/22 marks)

■ ■ ■

C-grade answer

Stalin used purges to control the USSR, but this was not the only way he attempted to control the country.

The Great Purge began in 1936 and lasted until 1938. In 1936 Stalin concentrated on the Communist Party, and leading figures such as Kamenev and Zhdanov were put on trial and shot for disloyalty to the party and treason.

The following year, it was the turn of the armed forces to suffer. Leading generals such as Trotsky were executed. Seven other top generals were executed in that year. Other top communists such as Radek were also killed in 1937.

In 1938, more top leaders of the Communist Party were purged. These included Bukharin and his followers. Bukharin went to his death praising the qualities of Stalin.

By now, Stalin had a lot of control and had got rid of most of his main rivals. Most of the top men in the Communist Party were now dead.

Soon no one was safe from Stalin. The secret police extended their arrests to ordinary people. A lot of arrests happened without even Stalin knowing about them. People used to denounce their neighbours and even family members. It was a terrible time.

However, it wasn't just terror that Stalin used to control the people of the USSR. He also used propaganda.

Stalin had a personality cult. Twenty-four provinces were named after him. His picture was everywhere, and there were statues of him in all the major cities and towns. The national anthem was changed to include Stalin. He had numerous flattering titles. A lot of songs and poems were written about Stalin too.

Stalin also used *Pravda* for propaganda. This was the Communist Party newspaper. It was a strong weapon of propaganda.

There was also a lot of censorship carried out by Stalin. It took place in the writing of history — which was to glorify Stalin's role in the Revolution — and philosophy. Artists and writers were expected to follow the party line to the letter.

Stalin also tried to create a Stalinist culture. Early on, a cultural revolution took place, where priests were attacked and writers and artists were put under pressure. In the arts, Soviet Realism was introduced. This meant giving simple messages in the arts which would keep away from complex ideas that Stalin mistrusted. Churches were closed down.

Therefore, while terror was very important for Stalin, propaganda and culture also helped him keep control over the USSR. They sent out a strong message and encouraged many to support him.

> **Overall: This answer attempts to develop points and to give evidence of statements made. It is balanced, with attention given to both the proposition and other factors, such as propaganda. It is focused, but more detail is needed, for example on the purges, Socialist Realism and the personality cult. It also includes occasional inaccuracy, for example on the Great Purge, and it is not always clear, for example on the persecution of religion.** (14/22 marks)